REVIVAL THAT REMAINS

Faith, soulwinning,
and missions in action!

Rick Aldridge

Remember the former things of old:
FOR *I am God, and there is none else;*
I am God, and there is none like Me.

Is. 46:9

**The primary purpose of remembering
is to recall that there is none like God.**

*The acknowledgement of what God has done
in the past through the churches, schools, ministries,
and individuals named does not necessarily
constitute an endorsement of these ministries
as they currently exist.*

REVIVAL THAT REMAINS

TABLE OF CONTENTS

Preface

Numerous scriptures admonish us to *remember.* Indeed, major portions of the Bible are historical. These inspired passages document what God did in order that we may remember. This begs the question, *why* does God put an emphasis on remembering? In my opinion, Isaiah 46:9 summarizes the answer to that question. *Remember the former things of old: for I am God, and there is none else. I am God, and there is none like Me.* God would have us to forget all that would either discourage us or lift us up with pride. God would have us to forget all that would create bitterness in us or that would tempt us to rest on our laurels. But God would have us to remember all that helps us to know that (He) *is God, and there is none else.* (He) *is God, and there is none like* (Him).

In February 2013 evangelist Mike Pelletier came to Eastern North Carolina for revival services at Freedom Baptist Church in Havelock. Brother Pelletier was also attempting to organize "Evangelistic Prayer Bands" across the nation. He called for a meeting of local pastors, and several of us convened at Calvary Baptist Church in nearby New Bern. Brother Pelletier shared his burden for groups across our nation to regularly pray for revival. Pastor Bill Wingard, the host pastor at Calvary Baptist, spoke up with the intention of encouraging the brethren to pray. He told of a revival that occurred in New Bern in 1958 and commented that "**to some extent, that revival continues until this day**." This book started out as an attempt to tell the story of that revival which has continuing effects. But, needless to say, the power of God was not restrained to only New Bern and Calvary Baptist Church. The scope of the book quickly grew to involve much more than just that one revival meeting in one town.

My desire is that God may use this book to do that which Brother Pelletier originally desired, that is, to stir our hearts to pray for revival again. In his book, <u>Revival and Revivalism</u>, Iain Murray comments: "...where such a spirit of prayer exists it is a sign that God is already intervening to advance His cause." May God intervene in the heart of every reader to advance His cause through prayer. As He does, revival will have already begun in our hearts.

Anyone who reads some of the accounts of the great revivals of the past will probably quickly note that most authors struggle with identifying exactly when and how a revival began. When the embers first begin to glow and the flames first begin to spread, it is often on a relatively small scale. Few take note of it, and therefore the events are scarcely documented. Sometimes a writer will identify a certain prayer warrior or group of prayer warriors and declare quite dogmatically that their prayers were the beginning of the revival but the writer may or may not be correct in crediting those individuals for being the human instruments that God used to bring revival to an area. Only God knows who He chose to use in getting revival fires burning. This fact is in keeping with the character of God and the value He places on humility. Who among us wouldn't be tempted with pride if we knew we had been greatly used of God to bring revival?

Having said that, this book will attempt to document some of the great things God has done in Eastern North Carolina over the past few decades by somewhat arbitrarily selecting a man named

Norman Pollard as a starting point. There is an appropriate irony in his name because Norm was not a pastor, preacher, or great spiritual leader of any well-known activity. Norm was a "normal" Christian, a lay person, a Sunday School teacher, a deacon, and later a chairman of the deacons. But this "normal" Christian had an abnormal passion for souls, and he also had the mighty power of God upon his witnessing efforts. Matthew Bateman grew up in People's Baptist Church of Greenville, North Carolina where Norm Pollard served for over five decades. Matthew said of Norm Pollard, "He was just a normal man... when you met him, when you saw him, he was just a plain old guy."

The other key person in this book whose memories are recorded is Pastor Bill Wingard of Calvary Baptist Church in New Bern. Most of the people mentioned in this book were either won to the Lord or directly influenced by Norman Pollard or Bill Wingard.

This book is primarily the result of dozens of personal interviews. Occasionally, as God's precious servants recalled the events of decades past, their memories would not quite agree in some detail. In areas where memories are inconsistent or poorly documented, the book is intentionally left vague.

Chapter One
Clyde Eborn Saved

It was big news in 1953 when the E.I. DuPont company chose to place the world's first plant devoted to the commercial production of polyester fiber just outside of rural Kinston, North Carolina. Tobacco had long been the economic driver in this area, so DuPont's investment of $40 million in production facilities and an additional $3 million investment in a lab sent out shock waves. Even the *New York Times* ran an article on March 24, 1953, which stated: "E.I. DuPont de Nemours Co., Inc. stepped into second gear yesterday in the production of its new polyester "Dacron" fiber. Production of the fiber was begun at the new $40,000,000 plant which DuPont has erected at Kinston, North Carolina, and the so-called pilot operation for Dacron output at Seaford, Delaware, is being shut down."

But what neither DuPont nor anyone else knew in 1953 was that something much greater than making a significant financial impact on a community was happening. DuPont was setting the infrastructure in place for a quiet but zealous soul winner to interact with people he likely never would have met otherwise, and several of those people would go on to be greatly used by God.

That soul winner was named Norm Pollard. Pollard had grown up extremely poor in the home of his single mother. They lived in a camper parked behind a country store in the tiny community of Belvoir, North Carolina. They had no electricity all the way into Pollard's high school years; Pollard did his homework by candlelight. Belvoir was listed as consisting of all of 307 souls in the 2010 census. No doubt, it was even smaller in 1931 when Pollard was born. It is located just outside of the larger city of Greenville, North Carolina, which is the home of East Carolina University. After a while, Norm's uncle moved in with them so that he could help his sister raise the boy. When Norm got old enough, he would cut wood or do small jobs for local farmers in order to help support his family.

Norm grew up with little to no Christian influence in his life. Leaning toward the wild side, he found an outlet in boxing. But by the grace of God, He accepted Christ as his Saviour at an Oliver B. Greene tent revival near Greenville, North Carolina. His son, Norman Ray, remembers that his father got saved shortly after Norman Ray was born in 1953, but unfortunately the story of exactly how Norman Pollard ended up being in that tent revival has been lost to history. Many souls can thank God for the unnamed hero of the faith who influenced Pollard to attend that tent revival.

He would later become a charter member of People's Baptist Church in Greenville in 1962, but as a new Christian in 1953 Pollard was just getting his feet wet. DuPont hired Pollard, and he began attending church. His duties as a guide inspector at the factory gave him occasion to move freely throughout the plant and enabled him to talk to many different people.

Another local boy that DuPont hired was fresh out of the Army and newlywed. Clyde Eborn had served a little over two years in Germany during the time of the Korean conflict. He got married in 1954, and the Holy Spirit was working on him to be saved; but he had not yet surrendered to the Spirit's call.

One day as Eborn was working in the DuPont production area, Pollard came by. Clyde was operating a machine and was decked out with all the required safety equipment including hard hat and ear plugs. By God's divine timing, Clyde just "happened" to have stepped away from his noisy machine for a moment. Clyde and Pollard didn't know each other very well at that time, but over the din of the production equipment Norm Pollard asked: "Are you a Christian?"

Eborn responded, "Working on it."

Pollard then asked, "Are you making any headway?"

Clyde simply replied, "Not sure."

Even though Pollard had only been saved a short while himself, he handed Clyde a copy of a tract entitled, "What Must I Do to Be Saved?" He then moved on toward the next stop on his rounds. Next to the Bible, this particular tract became Pollard's weapon of choice; and he would go on to hand out thousands of them over his lifetime. As a boy, Pollard's son remembers greeting the mailman and repeatedly hauling boxes of the tracts into the house. Some of the tracts and other literature that Norm Pollard handed out over the years were provided by churches he served in, but many were paid for from the Pollard family budget.

Clyde Eborn had shoved his copy of the tract into his pocket. Later, that day, he went into the restroom and read the answers to the question: What Must I Do to Be Saved? The tract had been written by the editor of the *Sword of the Lord* paper, John R. Rice. It was subtitled: "The Plan of Salvation Made Plain to Sinners from the Word of God." The first thing Eborn read was John R. Rice's pointed introduction. Rice wrote: "What must I do to be saved? Here in the simplest, shortest form is put the question to which every man must learn the answer, or spend eternity lost, away from God, suffering the torments of the damned!"

Dr. Rice then went on to highlight how the Philippian jailor had asked *What must I do to be saved?* in Acts 16:29-31. He expounded on the answer to the question: In order to be saved a person must see himself a sinner, he must see that Christ died to save sinners, "not good men." He must believe on the Lord Jesus Christ. In his concise, pointed style, Rice went on to emphasize that salvation is *not of works* and that it does require faith in the shed blood of Christ. He briefly discussed repentance, prayer, and confession, incorporating several Bible examples of each as he expounded.

The concluding point in the tract was: "Make It Sure - Claim Him Today!" The Bible passages that followed emphasized the brevity of life. *Boast not thyself of to morrow: for thou knowest not what a day may bring forth* (Proverbs 27:1), *Behold, now is the accepted time; behold, now is the day of salvation* (II Corinthians 6:2), *To day if ye will hear His voice, harden not your hearts* (Hebrews 3:7-8).

There, in a restroom in a noisy production plant just outside Kinston, North Carolina, Clyde Eborn bowed his head and asked the Lord to save him, and God did! What a humble beginning for someone who would go on to be so greatly used of God! Clyde excitedly told foks that he was a new man, but some who knew him well were skeptical.

Time quickly revealed that indeed Clyde Eborn was a new creature in Christ Jesus. Even though he was a new Christian, Clyde almost immediately began to partner with Norm Pollard in his soul

4

winning efforts. Pollard's son, Norman Ray Jr., remembers, "When they turned their life over to the Lord back then, it was 100%."

Like Norm, Clyde would earn the reputation of being a soul winner first, then being known according to his other roles in life. God richly blessed their efforts. Before Eborn resigned from DuPont a short time later, he and Norm Pollard would be able to tally up over 20 men who had gotten saved from the factory.

But when God is working, there is always opposition. Many were getting saved at DuPont, but others complained about their soul-winning efforts. One day, Clyde's supervisor, Tom, told him, "We didn't hire you to preach." Later that same day Tom came back by, and said, "You're fired. We're not going to need you anymore." Eborn calmly responded: "My wife's not going to like that. I'll see you tomorrow." Eborn came to work the next day, talked to the right people, and kept his job. Later, Tom fired him again, but Clyde never lost a day's work or a day's pay.

But Clyde was suffering physically. He had developed bleeding ulcers and was having trouble sleeping. His doctor told him that getting off shift work may help him. The company graciously developed a new position for him, allowing him to be a "day relief" when other workers couldn't make it in. This new position gave him access to even more of the facility, but it was a demanding job. He had to learn the duties and safety regulations for multiple positions, but he diligently applied himself and did well; and he continued to hand out tracts and win souls.

One day, Tom came by again and said, "You need to go see the plant manager." Clyde feared he was going to be fired again, but this time from the top level. He called on his friends to pray.

When he went in, the plant manager said, "I understand you're a Christian."

Eborn replied, "Yes, sir."

"I understand you're leaving a lot of tracts around the facility."

"Yes, sir."

They talked for a while, and then ultimately the plant manager simply said, "Be careful."

When Clyde came out and everyone asked him how it went, Clyde just smiled and responded, "He just said, 'Be careful.'"

While all this was happening at DuPont in Kinston, Clyde was using his days off to help a childhood friend who now ran a laundry truck. The truck would pick up and deliver laundry to the Marines on board the base at Marine Corps Air Station (MCAS) Cherry Point. As they ate lunch and interacted with the Marines, Clyde began to be burdened for reaching the military with the gospel. He was actively serving with a church about an hour away in Kinston, but he sensed that God had something more in mind for him. One night he was praying around midnight and became aware of what it was that God wanted him to do. Slipping into the bedroom, he found his wife in bed crying. She also sensed that God was working. He told her, "Pumpkin, God's called me to preach. We're going to have to get out of this place sooner or later." When Clyde informed the boys at DuPont that God had called him to preach, they simply said, "Well, you've been preaching, just keep it up."

Clyde Eborn would go on to be greatly used of God in ways that he could never have imagined back then, but at DuPont God was still using the soul-winning efforts of Norm Pollard.

Chapter Two
1956 Robert Joyner Saved

Norm Pollard had a fire in his heart that burned 24 hours a day. His concern for souls emanated from him regardless of where he was or who he was with. By no means were his soul-winning efforts limited to his work place. In 1956, God would use the witnessing that Norm Pollard did in his daily car pool to win another soul to Himself.

In addition to Norm Pollard and Clyde Eborn, DuPont had hired a 21-year-old young man named Robert in their initial flood of hiring. Once again God used shift work at DuPont to accomplish a divine purpose. One of Robert's married co-workers was supposed to change shifts, but the shift change would conflict with his wife's schedule. Robert was single, so the coworker paid him $40 to change shifts in his place. Those two twenty dollar bills didn't just lead to a shift change for Robert; they led to an eternity change. The shift change forced him to switch car pools; and by divine coincidence, his assigned seat in the new carpool was in the back seat right between an old high school buddy named Danny and Norm Pollard.

Robert had lost touch with Danny after high school, and it turned out that Danny was saved. As Robert would later describe it, as he rode to DuPont between Danny and Norm, "they began to talk strange." They were talking about things like being "saved" and being "born again." Robert had never heard such talk. He listened and asked questions, lots of questions. Later they would tell him that he asked more questions than anyone they'd ever seen. But they patiently provided solid Bible answers to his avalanche of questions, and again the seeds sown by Norm Pollard and others took root. As a direct result of their witnessing, eventually Robert accepted Jesus Christ as his Lord and Saviour.

Robert Joyner quickly began to study his Bible and grow in the Lord. Within a short time, he was teaching the adult Sunday School class at Calvary Baptist Church in Greenville. In 1957, now married, he and his wife Dorothy became charter members of this church. By 1961, just five years after he had gotten saved, he was in the ministry preaching. He started his first church in the little community of Shelmerdine, North Carolina. He would go on to also start and pastor other churches as well. Norm Pollard occasionally joined him in soul-winning visitation to assist him in some of his church planting efforts.

After some time he relocated from the small towns around Greenville moving closer to the coast. He settled in a community known as Mill Creek, which sits on the banks of the Newport River about 17 miles southeast of MCAS Cherry Point. Due to its proximity to the Atlantic Ocean, the Newport River is approximately one mile wide at Mill Creek. When one looks to the southeast, it's almost five miles to the nearest land. In addition, most of the land to the north and east of Mill Creek is part of the Croatan National Forest. This setting suited Joyner well since he was an avid hunter and outdoorsman.

Unfortunately, Joyner didn't last long at the Mill Creek church. One man who would later become a deacon with Pastor Joyner at another church, explained his short stay at Mill Creek in somewhat blunt terms: "He insisted that the deacons attend church services, and they ran him off."

His expulsion from Mill Creek opened the door for Robert Joyner to settle into his life work. In 1978, after resigning the church at Mill Creek, he began to hold services in nearby Newport, North Carolina. A few folks left Mill Creek with him, and with them he started Community Baptist Church of Newport. They held their first meetings under an old military tent, and then rented the historic one room Boy Scout building in town. In a relatively short period of time, God opened doors to purchase property on Highway 70, which is the main corridor to all points east in this sector of coastal North Carolina. Marines from the base quickly responded to his fiery preaching and his love for the outdoors. The church began to grow.

Thanks in part to a soul-winning Marine Staff Sergeant named Teddy Fulfer, several single Marines were saved. They were happy to get out of the barracks and off the base to help manually clear trees from the property and to assist with construction of the new church building. Even though it had the potential to put his career in jeopardy, Teddy was quite aggressive in his soul-winning efforts. One Marine named Mike, who had just recently gotten saved, saw Teddy coming through the parking lot to follow up, and to recruit Marines to ride the bus to Community Baptist. Because Mike had a beer in his hand and was immediately convicted, he jumped inside a trash dumpster to hide from Teddy. Once again, God divinely orchestrated events. Teddy ran into someone else to witness to in the parking lot, and Mike was trapped inside the dumpster until Teddy finally left. Mike promptly put down the alcohol and eventually married Pastor Joyner's niece. Both he and his wife have matured into respected Christians who have been spiritual leaders in their respective roles in several churches as the Marine Corps moved them until Mike retired. SSgt. Fulfer got out of the Marine Corps and has served as a missionary in the Philippines for decades.

Those early efforts at winning the single Marines from base were so effective that some of them declared that the acronym CBC no longer stood for Community Baptist Church. They dubbed it the Community Bachelors' Church.

Community Baptist Church continued to grow steadily. Military families were constantly rotating out, but new ones would be saved and come in as well. The church survived a couple of church splits, but God continued to bless despite the occasional turmoil. Then, in the mid 90's it seemed that it was finally time for Community Baptist to take its turn in experiencing the revival fires that had been burning in different parts of Eastern North Carolina since the late '50's and the '60's. There was a fresh emphasis on prayer, attendance rocketed upward, buses were filled, people were being saved consistently, and there was a wonderful excitement and enthusiasm felt at each service. One visiting singer during that glorious time labeled Community Baptist as "the happening church."

In the midst of God's blessings there, Pastor Joyner published a very controversial book regarding Bible translations. Although Pastor Joyner had always preached only from the King James

Version, the book he wrote gave "incontestable proof that the King James Version is not perfect" as the Forward to the book worded it. The book ignored any discussion of which original language manuscripts should or should not be used, and simply addressed "problems" with the English wording. The Introduction to the book describes the book's approach as dealing only with "surface truth."

To some, it seemed that the book was a wet rain upon the revival fires burning at Community Baptist. The machinery continued to function, and for a short period of time some growth continued; but the leadership team at the church began to disintegrate. This time, there was no church split, there was no conflict, but key people simply began to find occasion to move on. The church was accustomed to military transfers, but now civilian leaders also moved out. Some relocated to care for aging family members. The associate pastor left to pastor another church. Some who were expected to stay in the area when their enlistment was over got out of the military and went back home or relocated to other areas to find civilian jobs. And as always, military transfers also took their toll.

Then Pastor Joyner's wife had a stroke and ultimately graduated to heaven in 1999. His subsequent dating and remarriage caused ripples in the church after her death. Things snowballed, and in 2007, after having suffered a stroke himself, Pastor Joyner retired at 72 years of age, much earlier than anyone had expected. Despite the controversies and turbulence, Community Baptist graciously took care of their founding pastor. He had served there for almost 30 years.

Not every success story finishes well; but thankfully, God wasn't through with Community Baptist. He sent in a new pastor to lead the church through that transitional time. There are two situations that cause many pastoral candidates to be leery of accepting a pastorate. One situation is when a church has known only one pastor for many years and the church doesn't know any way of doing business except for that previous pastor's way. The other situation is the prospect of taking the helm of a church which has experienced recent turmoil.

Pastor Ken Bartholomew came to Community Baptist knowing he was facing both of those situations. This was the second time in his ministry when he had followed behind Robert Joyner. Pastor Bartholomew came from Liberty Baptist Church in Snow Hill, North Carolina, which was one of the churches that Pastor Joyner had pastored previously. Pastor Bartholomew promptly engaged the church in a major remodeling program. That may not be the wisest thing to do in all such situations; but as it turned out, it was just the right thing to do for Community Baptist at that time and in that situation. As at the beginning, the people of the church came together, focusing on doing the manual labor needed to take the church forward one more step. Pastor Ken also brought in Brother Billy Knox, who had been his associate pastor in Snow Hill. When Pastor Bartholomew resigned a few years later, Brother Billy assumed the pastorate and the church once again moved forward for the cause of Christ.

In spite of some rough seas, the gospel ship sails on at Community Baptist Church, and "*to some extent, that revival continues until this day.*" Several preachers have been sent out by Community Baptist, including this author.

But, by no means was saving Robert Joyner the only thing God did in Eastern North Carolina in the late '50s. God had also found a servant to send to New Bern to preach a tent revival.

Chapter Three

1958 Calvary Baptist Church of New Bern Started

At 86 years old, Pastor Bill Wingard's mind was still incredibly sharp. He rattled off numerous names and dates with certainty as he recalled how wonderfully God had moved throughout his life and ministry. Yet, despite his excellent memory, Pastor Bill Wingard wasn't sure who the preacher was that came to New Bern and preached a tent revival in 1958. He thought it may have been the converted Jewish evangelist from White Russia named Hyman Appleman. Wingard was not in New Bern in 1958. He didn't arrive until 1962 when he became the pastor of Calvary Baptist Church, which started as an indirect result of the '58 revival. But Bill Wingard didn't seem to be overly concerned about who the preacher was. As he stated it: "It was not a preacher meeting. It was a God meeting; I mean everything about it was the Lord." He also mentioned that God greatly used Christian businessmen in the '58 revival.

Others remembered other revivals from those early years, but no one could say with certainty who held that tent revival that resulted in a nucleus of people coming together to form what later became Calvary Baptist Church of New Bern. Missionary Dalton Heath, also an Eastern North Carolina native, remembers the founder of the Word of Life and Youth for Christ ministries out of Schroon Lake, New York, Jack Wyrtzen, coming to New Bern about the same time and preaching a big revival in the historical New Bern Shriner's building. But Pastor Wingard seemed sure it was a tent meeting. Pastor Dennis Wiggs, long time pastor of Ruth's Chapel FWB Church, also in New Bern, felt pretty sure it was Hyman Appelman. Clyde Eborn spoke of a great revival meeting held in a tent where the preacher was a man named Johnny Flood, but after some consideration he determined that the Flood revival, where two of Eborn's brothers got saved, was sometime later than 1958. Some charter members of Calvary Baptist Church thought they remembered different speakers preaching during the revival, but they weren't certain.

Regardless of who did the preaching, God was working mightily. Many people were getting saved. Holy Ghost conviction seemed to be walking the streets of the city that had been North Carolina's first capital city. Being the first capital had already given New Bern some interesting religious history. It was from the Tryon Palace in New Bern that, during the Colonial Days, British Governor Tryon marched west with troops to squash the rebellion of the "Regulators." He strongly identified the Separate Baptists with the Regulators, and indeed there was a connection. The Separate Baptists were very supportive of the Regulators' opposition to taxation without representation. They also strongly opposed Governor Tryon's aggressive endorsement of the Church of England as the state church and the taxes he levied on the pioneers in support of this state church. The resulting Battle of Alamance, North Carolina, on May 16, 1771, is considered by some to be the opening salvo of the Revolutionary War.

But all of that was almost two centuries behind New Bern by 1958. Now, God was using the Baptists who were so despised by Governor Tryon to make a significant impression on the town. Some of New Bern's influential business leaders got saved.

Forest Minges, the owner of the local Pepsi distributor, was among them. Pepsi had been invented in New Bern by Caleb Bradham and was being publicly sold by 1898. Bradham became a millionaire, but then during World War I sugar prices skyrocketed from 5 cents to 22 cents per pound. Bradham invested heavily in futures contracts for sugar; but then the bottom dropped out, and sugar prices fell to 2-3 cents per pound. Bradham declared bankruptcy in 1923 and sold Pepsi. The new buyers reorganized, and Pepsi prospered once again. By 1958 Pepsi headquarters were in New York. The company's big advertising campaign that year was the introduction of their "swirl bottle."

Of course, Pepsi was being sold once again back in New Bern and was being distributed by the Minges bottling company. As will be seen later, Mr. Minges and his family would prove themselves to be real friends to Christian ministries.

Other key business leaders were getting saved also. The owner of WHIT, a local radio station, got saved. This would later open doors for WHIT to be the first station for Pastor Bill Wingard to air the Calvary Hour program. In turn, this radio work would later open doors for Pastor Wingard when it was time for him to be used by God in an even greater way, as will be seen in following chapters.

Businesses began opening their doors to preachers and allowing gospel services on their premises. Oettinger Brothers Furniture Company allowed soul winners to bring people in off the sidewalk and sit on their new display couches while the soulwinners led others to the Lord. It was from this group of people who were saved, blessed, or whose spirits were stirred by this city-wide 1958 revival that a nucleus of people formed what would become Calvary Baptist Church.

The fact that God is working wonderfully doesn't mean there won't be trouble. In fact, when God is working, it almost guarantees there will be trouble. The nucleus which would be the start of Calvary Baptist Church consisted of six families totaling about 30 people, but they were divided into four groups. One preacher worked with them for about a year, then left before formally becoming their pastor. Things got so ugly that at one point the preacher literally had to run into somebody's house to get away from some of them. After he left, the group began reaching out, looking for someone who would stay with them as pastor.

Somebody from the group wrote to Oliver B. Greene informing him that they needed a pastor in New Bern. Greene, in turn, passed the word on to Dr. Gilbert Stenholm who was Dean of the Department of Religion (but who Pastor Wingard referred to simply as "Dean of Preacher Boys"), at Bob Jones University. Bill Wingard was one of those "preacher boys." He had been saved after attending a soul winning class while serving as a Navy Corpsman in Portsmouth, Virginia. During the class he realized he'd never been born again himself, and he accepted Christ as his Saviour.

After his tour of duty in Virginia, the young Corpsman was assigned to the 1st Marine Division and transferred to Oceanside, California. There in the First Baptist Church of Oceanside, he and his wife Arlie were loved and discipled by Neil and Verline Glenn. Neil was also a Navy Corpsman. Under the tutelage of these mentors, Bill and Arlie Wingard won their first souls, taught their first classes, and grew in the Lord. Bill Wingard would later affectionately refer to Neil and Verline Glenn as the "Priscilla and Aquila" of his and Mrs. Arlie's lives.

But at this time, Bill Wingard was a student at BJU and was working on his doctorate. God began to work in his heart about this need in New Bern, North Carolina. After a period of prayer, the Wingard's drove to New Bern so that he could candidate for the position. This decision resulted in his failing to ever complete his doctorate, although later he would receive an honorary Doctorate of Humanities from Bob Jones University as well as an honorary Doctorate of Divinity from Heritage College of Orlando, Florida.

In New Bern, the pulpit committee grilled him, then allowed him to preach a sermon. After preaching that candidate sermon, they asked him, "What percentage of the vote is it going to take to bring you here? The nervous young preacher meant to say "A majority vote," but somehow what came out of his mouth was, "A unanimous vote." They looked at him like he was crazy, and someone said: "Man, nobody could get a unanimous vote here."

The church voted, and incredibly the divided new church did give the young candidate a unanimous vote. Bill Wingard became the pastor of Calvary Baptist Church. He had briefly pastored an outreach church in Pelham, South Carolina, while at Bob Jones; but that church and Calvary Baptist would be the only two churches he would ever pastor. For the first few weeks, Bill and Arlie Wingard commuted back and forth between Greenville, South Carolina, and New Bern, North Carolina. Today, with interstate highways and 70 mph speed limits the trip still takes approximately 6 1/2 hours. But in 1962, most interstate highways were only lines on Department of Transportation blueprints. The Federal-Aid Highway Act creating interstate highways had been signed into legislation in 1956, and by 1962 only a few short sections of interstate were open for traffic. With Interstate highways in their infancy, the trip from Greenville, South Carolina, to New Bern, North Carolina, was a very long day of travel through numerous small towns, and almost exclusively across two-lane roads.

Preacher Bill's first sermon as pastor of Calvary Baptist was "Why beholdest thou the mote in thy brother's eye?" After the service one of the men who would go on to become "his mortal enemy" angrily told him: "If you had preached like that last Sunday, you wouldn't be here today!" Those words set the ominous tone for the year ahead.

1963 was a tough year for the Wingard family. There was constant turmoil in the splintered little church group. Pastor Wingard sought counsel from advisors at Bob Jones and others. By this time, Clyde Eborn had become a close friend and a strong source of encouragement to Bill Wingard. At one point when Wingard was considering resigning, Eborn firmly told him: "Forget it, you're going nowhere. We prayed too hard to get you here. Settle down, we've got a job to do."

Despite the trouble at the fledgling Calvary Baptist Church, a spirit of revival was still percolating throughout New Bern. Businesses were still opening their doors to preachers and the gospel. The downtown Belk store allowed preachers to come in every Monday before business hours, and they allowed their employees to select and invite these guest preachers. A black gentleman named Mr. Hines operated the elevators for Belk. Pastor Wingard didn't know him personally, but apparently Hines had heard him preach on the radio and liked his preaching. Every time it was Mr. Hines's turn to invite a preacher, he invited Bill Wingard.

At the end of the first turbulent year at Calvary Baptist Church, Pastor Wingard did tender a letter of resignation with a one-month notice, in spite of Clyde Eborn's objections. A local newspaper interviewed him, and Preacher Bill told them, "You tell them I'm leaving Calvary, but I'm not leaving New Bern." Shortly before his death, Pastor Wingard chuckled heartily as he recalled the effect of that statement: "That was like throwing a possum in the hen house." But God wasn't through with him at Calvary Baptist.

The last Sunday before his resignation was to take effect arrived. Preacher Bill preached in the morning service, then went to a neighboring town to participate in an ordination service at another church. That afternoon, one of the leaders of Calvary Baptist called for a meeting. He asked, "How many of you are going to accept the preacher's resignation?" This question opened the floor for discussion and it soon became apparent that not everybody wanted Wingard to leave. After a while the brother suggested, "Why don't we do away with the deacons and let Pastor Wingard choose some men he can work with?" By a miraculous act of God, the church members agreed. When Pastor Wingard returned for his final message that Sunday evening, he found the church buzzing with excitement. Someone informed him of their decision and he agreed to stay. As it turned out he never did leave Calvary Baptist Church of New Bern until he was promoted to heaven on March 12, 2021.

The ring leader of the trouble in the church did leave Calvary Baptist Church and went to another church. Within six months he died from a massive heart attack. He was only 39 years old.

After it was established that "Preacher Bill" was going to remain as Pastor, Calvary Baptist Church experienced the full force of the embers of revival fires that had been smoldering since the 1958 tent revival. The church was blessed with about 27 months of perpetual revival. Many people were coming and getting saved. Sometimes they would baptize thirty people at a time.

The combined effects of the 1958 tent revival, the 27 months of revival in Calvary Baptist Church afterward, and the overall spirit of revival throughout New Bern and Eastern North Carolina are what prompted Bill Wingard to make the statement in the 2013 pastor's meeting, "***to some extent, that revival continues until this day.***"

Let's let Pastor Wingard tell in his own words one example of how the effects of that revival were still a very real blessing to Calvary Baptist Church amidst the COVID shutdowns of 2020:

"This just happened this week (the week of 11/19/20). One of the ladies that got saved was named E_____ R____. She was the daughter of K____ and I___ S____ who were here in New Bern.... She got saved and boy, she caught on fire for the Lord. Her husband worked for the FAA. She started witnessing to her family. Her Mama got saved and later her Daddy got saved. Her nephew that was involved in witchcraft, he got saved. His mother, that was as hard as nails, she got saved. A whole bunch of them got saved, and then they transferred with the FAA to Alabama and I lost track of them... this was 50 years ago or more. So, two Saturdays ago... I get a phone call and a lady says I'm K_____ S_____'s granddaughter and my Mama has been keeping up with your video services, and my Daddy also. He died, and now my Mama has died. My Mama wanted to give a gift to the church... and we children have decided that we're going to honor that and we're going to go ahead and give a gift."

Pastor Wingard then read from the note that they sent with the check. The note included the statement: "Her love for the Lord spread throughout our family and beyond." The note was signed by all the children, and the check was for $10,000. From just one lady that had gotten saved five decades previously, "Her love for the Lord spread throughout [that] family and beyond," and five decades later Calvary Baptist Church was still being blessed by the spirit of revival that remained in that family in 2020!

Doubtless such stories could be repeated dozens of times in multiple families. Revival is worth praying for! Thank God for those who prayed. Thank God for the brother who had the backbone to stand and lead the little group at Calvary Baptist to retain their preacher! Thank God for friends like Clyde Eborn who offer encouragement during hard times. Thank God that He saved that one precious lady during that time of revival!

That meeting held by an evangelist whose name has been lost to history in New Bern, North Carolina, wasn't the only example of God using an old-fashioned tent meeting. In nearby Greenville, North Carolina, and at about the same time, God was using another tent meeting to start another church. This time, the evangelist's name is very well-known.

Chapter Four
1962 People's Baptist
Church Started

Evangelist Oliver B. Greene brought his big green gospel tent to Eastern North Carolina many times. His tent revivals and his radio preaching on "The Gospel Hour" program had a tremendous impact on this portion of America. It has already been mentioned that Norman Pollard was saved in one of those tent revivals in the early 50s. One of the places where Greene would set up his tent periodically was near Greenville, North Carolina. In the book When God Is In It, Greene's song leader and brother-in-law J. Bennett Collins tells how a tornado tore down the tent in one of those Greenville meetings. The revival had to be concluded in a nearby ball park. Thankfully, no one was seriously injured in the storm and some folks still got saved in the open-air meeting in the ball field.

Greene's strong preaching on the eternal security of the believer was one factor which caused a group of believers to pull out primarily from Free Will Baptist churches they were attending and to start a new church which better represented what they had come to believe; that indeed believers *are sealed unto the day of redemption* as it is worded in Ephesians 4:30. Norm Pollard united with this group. Several people who shared their memories of him commented on the fact that every time he had an opportunity to teach or testify publicly, or even to pray, he would comment on being thankful that he was eternally secure in Christ. Pastor Max Barton was Norm's pastor at People's from 1989 until Norm graduated to heaven in 2008. Pastor Barton laughed as he remembered, "Every time he gave a devotion or taught a Sunday School class, he would get off on eternal security. Every time!"

These strong convictions lead this group of believers to organize a new church in Greenville, North Carolina. At first, they named it People's Bible Church. Over the years, the name would change to People's Baptist Temple; and then in 1993, under Pastor Barton's leadership, the name was changed to People's Baptist Church. For the sake of simplicity, the church will be referred to simply as People's, or as People's Baptist Church, throughout the remainder of this book.

The new church originally met in the home of Mr. and Mrs. Dennis Sutton until they secured a rented facility. Brother Chester Fussell, a lifetime resident of Pitt County except for a stint as an Army Medical Corpsman in WWII, preached for them until they asked a preacher named Jack Mosher to come hold a revival. The revival led to Mosher becoming the first pastor of People's. Chester Fussell continued in the ministry, starting several churches, and winning many to the Lord.

God greatly used Jack Mosher, and the fledgling church prospered under his leadership. Many souls were saved and discipled. When they were ready to charter, Dr. Harold Sightler assisted in writing their bylaws. Sightler served as the pastor of the Tabernacle Baptist Church in Greenville, South Carolina. He also hosted the Bright Spot Hour radio program which he had begun in 1943. This radio program would eventually be aired on over 100 stations coast to coast. Even though he was pastoring, he was highly sought after to hold evangelistic meetings, and God used him to serve as a mentor to many young preachers including those in Eastern North Carolina.

When they were ready to begin supporting missionaries, Oliver B. Greene was the very first preacher that People's Bible Church took on to support. Jack Mosher will be mentioned several times in the following chapters. He remained with them for four years, but then in 1966 he shocked everyone by moving to California to go into business and by eventually dropping out of the ministry altogether.

There was a healthy emphasis on "youth meetings" in those early days. Different churches in Eastern North Carolina would host events, and youth leaders would take their young people to the meetings. At People's, charter member Dave Woodard and his young wife Lou worked with the youth until the church grew to the point it could hire a full time youth pastor. Several of the people interviewed from the different churches commented on the good memories they had of those early get togethers. It's inconceivable how that such a practice has almost died out even though all who spoke of its past spoke favorably. Apparently as each church grew, it expended more of its energies and resources inwardly.

In 1967, John Woodley became the second pastor at People's. Woodley was an 82nd Airborne veteran who, like Bill Wingard, had answered the call to preach and had attended BJU with the assistance of G.I. Bill benefits. By the time Woodley became pastor, Norm Pollard was one of the deacons; but the deacons and Woodley didn't always see things the same way. Later, Pollard would serve as chairman of the deacons while Max Barton pastored People's Baptist from 1989 till Pollard graduated to heaven in 2008. Barton would remember Pollard as a deacon who was "always for the pastor, and the pastor's vision; and he shared the vision that the pastor presented to the church. He was eager in seeing those things get accomplished." But in those early years, during Woodley's tenure, there was disagreement between the pastor and the deacons.

During this time there was a great demand for Christian schools to provide an alternative to all that was happening in the public schools. Pastor Woodley was in favor of starting a Christian school, but Pollard and the other deacons were hesitant for the young church to assume the financial responsibilities associated with a school. People's had acquired their own property by then, and so finally a compromise was reached. Woodley and others organized a Christian school as a separate non-profit entity which assumed all financial responsibilities, but with the agreement that they could use the church property. In this way, Greenville Christian Academy began in 1969 with 110 students in grades K-4. Each year the school added a grade until they graduated their first three seniors in 1977. John Woodley stayed with People's until 1974, but the friction between him and the deacons never entirely dissipated. In '74 he resigned the church. Eleven families left People's at the same time, and started a new church nearby. The splinter group eventually called Woodley to be their pastor. He stayed there at Landmark Baptist until he retired 25 years later in 1998.

After Pastor Woodley left, People's Baptist Church absorbed Greenville Christian Academy and it became a ministry of the church rather than a separate entity. Thankfully, the academy has prospered and *continues to this day* with a 2021-2022 enrollment of 287 students. The school has graduated over 800 students since its inception. One of those graduates is Matthew Bateman. He knew Norm Pollard well and was quoted in the Preface. Both Matthew and his son Gavin have entered the ministry.

Despite the roller coaster ride of the early years at People's, oscillating between God's blessings and unexpected pastor resignations, the church continued to grow and prosper. Other pastors came and went; and Norman Pollard faithfully served under each one, eventually becoming the chairman of the deacons just before Pastor Max Barton arrived in 1989. When Pollard's health began to fail so that he could no longer actively serve as a deacon, the church voted to make him a deacon emeritus. Brother Barton was there in 2008 for Pollard's homegoing and preached Pollard's funeral along with Rev. Ernie Mills of the Durham Rescue Mission. One of his last acts of service to the church was to help train the new chairman of the deacons, Harold Stiltner. Brother Stiltner also remembered Norm Pollard as "a pastor's deacon."

This aspect of the revival started in Oliver B. Greene's tent and resulted in People's Baptist Church, and "*that revival continues until this day.*" People's Baptist Church is still a strong, vibrant church in the Greenville area. The church continues to effectively reach the young people in this college town, and they are still strongly missions minded, donating over $300,000 to missions in 2021.

God was still using Norm Pollard as he continued to work at DuPont and serve the Lord through People's Baptist Church. God also had big plans for one of the young men Pollard had been influential in leading to the Lord. It was time for Clyde Eborn to move toward the coast.

Chapter Five
1962 Grace Baptist of Morehead City Started

From that point, when Clyde Eborn surrendered to the ministry, God began to move. Clyde felt sure God wanted him to move closer to the base to work with the military, but he didn't have specific guidance on whether to go to Havelock which was just outside the base, Newport a few miles east, or Morehead City which was approximately 20 miles from MCAS Cherry Point. In 1962, God opened the door for them to start a church in Morehead City. With the help of an uncle and another family, a building was rented. In the first month, they scraped together enough money to buy chairs, a piano, and their first bus. They started the first independent Baptist church in Carteret County and named it Grace Baptist Church.

A one-legged man named Brother Wood soon got saved. Brother Wood helped them clean out the old bus they had bought from the state, and Pastor Eborn drove that first bus himself. His wife ran a second route, picking up people in either their VW bug or their Corvair. They put an air horn on the bus. They would visit on Saturdays and tell people, "When you hear the air horn, come out and get on the bus."

A man named Walter began to come on Sunday mornings. Finally, he showed up for a Sunday night service, and he got saved the first Sunday night that he attended. Pastor Eborn told him "I'm going to make a bus driver out of you," but Walter wasn't the least bit interested. Pastor Eborn told him, "It's simple, you just blow the air horn and people come out and get on the bus." Walter did become their bus driver, but the air horn generated a lot of complaints from those who liked to sleep late on Sunday mornings, and they finally had to stop using it.

The bus ministry continued to grow and would go on to run as many as ten routes. Grace Baptist Church has reached thousands of families over the 60+ years they have run buses.

Finally, the time came for Clyde Eborn to resign from DuPont in order to pastor full time. Tom, the supervisor who had fired him twice, told him: "Just before you starve to death, come back and see me." Years later, when he got word that Tom was sick, Brother Eborn went to visit him. He reminded Tom that he hadn't been back to beg for his old job. After a period of reminiscing, Clyde Eborn had the privilege of leading Tom to the Lord. Tom had been a Catholic, but he placed his faith solely in Jesus Christ as his Lord and Saviour shortly before he died.

With souls being saved constantly, Grace Baptist Church was growing and needed more room. The oil company they were renting from allowed them to build a small extension on the building but with the stipulation that they had to restore the building to its original configuration when they left. That extension room that they built and then later removed remains on the campus of Grace Baptist Church to this day. It was at a revival here in this one room rented building that a young preacher named Russell Bell would first meet Bill Wingard. The three preachers, Eborn, Wingard, and Bell would go on to form a friendship that was favored by God, and used to further His kingdom.

Grace Baptist Church needed their own property. Pastor Eborn had Harold Sightler to come in from Greenville, South Carolina, to preach. In Morehead City, Pastor Eborn took Brother Sightler to the site of five acres they had been praying about. As a young preacher, Eborn expected Sightler to pray a long impassioned prayer on behalf of the church. Instead, still seated in the car, Harold Sightler simply closed his eyes and said, "Lord you know the need of this young preacher and the church property. If you want him to have it, give it to him." They got it.

Grace Baptist Church continued doing well, growing, seeing souls saved and baptized. Church attendance peaked at over 1,000 on a big day. The church was now running numerous buses and had a "100 Club." Bus captains who brought in over a hundred on their route got their name put on a plaque and then the plaques were hung in the hallway. Several bus captains achieved this century mark.

The friendship between Pastors Eborn and Wingard continued to grow. At one point the churches competed in a "Crow Eating Contest." They chose a Sunday and agreed that the pastor of the church which had the least visitors on that day would have to eat fried crow. Calvary Baptist in New Bern lost the contest, so someone shot a crow, a lady in the church fried it, and Pastor Wingard prepared to take a bite. Just before he picked it up, Pastor Eborn snatched it off his plate and ate it instead.

Grace Baptist Church sold bonds to raise money and began to build on the property that Harold Sightler had helped pray them into. Things went well until it came time to put the rafters on. With most of the rafters in place, something broke on the first truss and all the rafters fell. There was no high wind or any obvious reason for the structure to give, but it did. One young man fell from the wall in the process, and had to be taken to the hospital for a checkup. Thankfully there were no injuries.

They had to start over. They got all the rafters back in place, and a crane was loading the plywood for the roof when suddenly the rafters fell a second time. This time the combined weight of the falling rafters and the plywood caused one of the outside walls to pull in. Once again, they had to clean up the mess, plus this time they had to hook come-a-longs to trees and trucks in order to straighten and then reinforce the damaged wall. Once that was completed the decision was made to switch to steel rafters although they were much more expensive. After a period of time, the building was completed and they could hold church services in their new auditorium.

Later they would build a tee on the building for classrooms in anticipation of Grace Christian School. The school was started in 1970 and continued for fifty years. It was finally shut down in 2020 due to declining enrollment during the COVID pandemic. The church chose to embrace and help facilitate home schooling instead.

An example of how "*to some extent, that revival continues until this day*" can be seen in one product of that bus ministry that had begun with an air-horned bus and a Corvair. In 1978 Marine Staff Sergeant Frank Basdeo returned to Marine Corps Air Station Cherry Point after a tour of duty in Okinawa, Japan. Frank and his family began moving in to their base housing on Monday. Saturday morning, bus workers from Grace Baptist Church of Morehead City knocked on their door. The next Saturday, different bus workers came knocking. On the third Saturday, the knock came again but this time the bus worker's team included a corporal who had worked for SSgt. Basdeo in Okinawa. Corporal Les Bolton had been somewhat of a rough character in Okinawa, but SSgt. Basdeo could see a change in him now. This time Frank agreed to go to church but said that if anyone was going to take his girls to church it would be him. He would drive.

They did attend church that Sunday, and he was shocked when he walked in and the usher gave him a friendly greeting and called him by name. Three or four others also welcomed him and called him by name even though they'd never met.

Monday, Mrs. Eborn went to the Basdeo's home and led Frank's wife, Mrs. Pauline Basdeo, to the Lord. A week went by and then Pauline said, "There's a revival at church; I'd like to go." Frank replied, "Go on, just leave me alone." At that point he didn't even know what a revival was. Tuesday, Pauline wanted to go to church again. Frank was incredulous. "They're having church AGAIN?! On a Tuesday night? In the end, he went with her that Tuesday night. Evangelist Dolphus Price was preaching the revival; and on that Tuesday night, June 6, 1978, Frank Basdeo went forward and accepted Jesus Christ as his Lord and Saviour.

Within a couple months, Frank became involved in the bus ministry. Since he lived in base housing, he was assigned to work with one of the base bus routes. He continued working the route until he had to pull another tour of duty in Okinawa, but he worked a bus route there as well while he attended Maranatha Baptist Church. When he returned to Cherry Point in '83, the bus director at Grace was moving away, so they asked Brother Frank to be the new bus director. Apart from some additional overseas deployments before he retired as a Master Sergeant in 1991, Frank Basdeo has continuously served as the bus director at Grace Baptist Church. He was 75 years old when interviewed, yet his youthful enthusiasm for the bus ministry is absolutely contagious.

"*That revival continues until this day*" in numerous ways. Brother Frank easily rattles off names of numerous men who he still maintains contact with who were saved through the bus ministry and are now actively serving the Lord in other places. One of the Basdeo's daughters graduated from Crown College with a degree in education. His older daughter became a registered nurse and married a Marine who would later become the assistant pastor at Grace Baptist Church.

Brother Frank and his wife are originally from Trinidad. Five of his six sisters have been saved and are serving the Lord. All this and more has happened because some persistent bus workers wouldn't give up on the possibility of two little five and seven-year-old girls riding the bus back in 1978!

The salvation of Brother Charles Tyler provides another example of how that "*to some extent, that revival continues until this day.*" Charles was a local boy who was playing guitar in a band. A friend who attended Grace Baptist Church kept inviting him to church, but he never went. But then, Charles was in a horrible van crash with the other members of the band as they were returning from playing a gig at a bar in Virginia. After surviving the crash,

Charles told his wife Candy that he was going to church. They both went to Grace Baptist Church and got saved.

That next weekend Charles was torn. He had made a commitment to play guitar for the band, and they were scheduled to perform at a bar in South Carolina. He knew that as a Christian, he shouldn't go; but he also felt strongly that he should keep his word and not let the band down without giving them notice that he was quitting. Shortly before leaving for South Carolina, they heard the phone inside the house ring. The van driver wanted to ignore it and get on the road, but Charles insisted someone go answer the phone. The call informed them that the bar in South Carolina had burned down and their services wouldn't be needed! Charles Tyler notified the band members that he was quitting. He went on to attend Tennessee Temple University, and then to become a pastor. He has used his carpentry skills to be a great blessing to each church he has pastored in Eastern North Carolina.

God was greatly using all the efforts at Grace Baptist Church, but the fact that Clyde Eborn had moved on from DuPont didn't slow down his coworker's soul winning efforts at all. Norm Pollard and others were still everlastingly at it and were making an impact.

Chapter Six
1964 Ernie Mills Saved

It was an uncomfortable experience when a nineteen-year-old boy named Ernie walked into People's Baptist of Greenville on June 7, 1964. Ernie's Dad was a poor sharecropper and a caring father who provided for his family, but he was an alcoholic. His father had died of cirrhosis of the liver in 1960 at only 40 years old. Ernie was still troubled over the loss of his Dad and was feeling the weight of the responsibilities that had been thrust upon him as a teenager due to his father's death. On top of that, church was new to him. Growing up in the home of an alcoholic had provided him with no religious background whatsoever.

Ernie, his sister Ellen, and his brother-in-law had found their way to church that morning because a young preacher, who was yet another DuPont employee, came through their neighborhood on door-to-door visitation. Frank Smith had knocked on Ellen's mobile home door and had invited her and her husband Richard to revival services at People's Baptist. They had given him their word that they would come, not to the revival services, but they promised they would come on Sunday. For some reason Frank did not go next door and invite Ernie, but stopped his visitation for that day at Ellen's home. However, Ellen promptly went next door and insisted that her brother Ernie go with them. Ernie laughs now, remembering that he got saved because a sinner invited him to church. He also laughs as he tells of how he teased Brother Smith over the years because Frank failed to come next door and invite him to church. Brother Frank would go on to start and pastor several churches in Eastern North Carolina over six decades of ministry. After retirement, Frank Smith once again served as a member of People's Baptist Church until his homegoing in 2022.

One of the first people to greet Ernie and his sister as they entered the church that Sunday was Norman Pollard. He loved people and was a natural fit for the greeter's job. He had a warm and ready smile that helped visitors feel at home right away. But Norm was doing more than just greeting people, he was also reading them as they came in. He would pray that God would lead him to those who were hurting or were spiritually needy. So, it was no accident that when the church service began, Norm Pollard "just happened" to be seated right behind Ernie Mills.

A preacher named Dale Fasenfell was preaching the revival messages. Fifty-eight years later, Ernie Mills had no recollection of what the preacher preached on that morning, but he did remember one thing very distinctly. By the end of the sermon, he knew that he was a sinner, he needed to get saved, and if he died, he'd go to hell.

But Ernie Mills didn't want to get saved. He was under the impression that Christians never had a good time. As a new high school graduate who was enrolled to study electrical engineering at Pitt Community College, he was looking forward to the college life. The congregation stood to sing an invitational hymn, and Ernie felt the weight of Holy Ghost conviction so strongly he thought he was going to pass out. He sat down while everyone else remained standing and singing. Suddenly, someone patted him on his shoulder and whispered, "Charles, don't you want to go forward and accept Christ?" (as a child they called Ernie by his middle name, probably to distinguish him from his father Ernest). Ernie violently shook his head and said, "No!" His sister and brother-in-law had already gone forward to be saved, but Ernie was determined. He was not going forward. Instead, he willed himself to stand back up with those singing the invitation.

He didn't stay standing long. Again, the weight of the Holy Ghost conviction weighed so heavily that it seemed impossible to stand. He sat back down. Again, Norm Pollard gently tapped him on the shoulder and asked, "Charles, don't you want to be saved?" This time Ernie humbly replied, "Yes sir."

Norm Pollard took him into a side room to the right of the pulpit and walked Ernie down the Romans Road.

As it is written, There is none righteous, no not one.
                                    Romans 3:10

For all have sinned, and come short of the glory of God;
                                    Romans 3:23

For the wages of sin is death; but the gift of God is eternal life through Jesus Christ our Lord.
                                    Romans 6:23

But God commendeth His love toward us, in that, while we were yet sinners, Christ died for us.
                                    Romans 5:8

That if thou shalt confess with thy mouth the Lord Jesus, and shalt believe in thine heart that God hath raised Him from the dead, thou shalt be saved.... For whosoever shall call upon the name of the Lord shall be saved.

Romans 10:9, 13

On June 7, 1964, Ernie Mills prayed with Norm Pollard and asked Jesus Christ to be his Lord and Saviour.

Norm Pollard gave him a Bible and wrote the date in the Bible, a fact that Ernie is thankful for. He likely would have forgotten the exact date otherwise, although he never would have forgotten the event. Ernie went back to church Sunday night and Wednesday night. On that Wednesday night Norm Pollard approached him and said, "Charles, I'm going visiting Friday. Wouldn't you like to come with me?" Ernie didn't have a clue what it meant to go visiting, but he knew this man loved him and cared for his soul, so he wanted to spend more time with Norm Pollard. He wanted to learn from Norm, so he said yes he would go.

Pollard continued, "Oh, by the way, could you just memorize Romans 3:23 between now and Friday?" As the soft-spoken Ernie Mills told this story 58 years later, he suddenly clapped his hands and raised his voice so loud it was startling. He laughingly exclaimed: "That rascal, he was discipling me already! I'm just four days old in the Lord, and now he's discipling me in the Lord!" Pollard then asked to see Ernie's Bible, and in the margin beside Romans 3:10, he wrote 3:23, then beside Romans 3:23, he wrote 5:8, then he mapped the way to 6:23, and 10:9-13. He told Mills "Now, you don't have to memorize all these verses right now." But Pollard got Ernie started on memorizing the Romans Road the first week Ernie was saved.

Friday night came and Pollard told Ernie, "You won't have to say a word. I'll do the talking. You just pray for me as I talk to the people we visit." Mills responded, "I can keep my mouth shut." Norm Pollard took Ernie out about three or four times, then he said, "You've seen me lead two or three people to the Lord now, and you know the verses; why don't you do the talking, and I'll pray for you as you talk to this person." For two or three weeks Pollard encouraged the young Ernie to do the talking on some of the visits; then one night it happened. Ernie led his first soul to Christ.

As Mills described this night, the 77 year old once again abruptly switched from his soft-spoken self into an explosion of energy. Throwing his hands into the air like a referee signaling a touchdown, he shouted, "Whew! You talk about excitement! Knowing that God used this old sinner to show somebody else how to be saved and on their way to heaven!" The soul winning and revival fires that motivated Norm Pollard had been lit in Ernie Mills. To the glory of God that revival *continues until this day!*

Ernie continued going on soul-winning visitation. That next month he announced his call to preach; and Pastor Jack Mosher, who was a BJU graduate, encouraged him to switch his enrollment from Pitt Community College to Bob Jones University. In those days when Bob Jones Sr. was still alive, BJU was the preferred university for most fundamentalists. Ernie followed his pastor's advice, and in September he found himself a student at Bob Jones University.

Don't miss how quickly things happened here. Ernie Mills graduated high school in May, got saved in June, led his first soul to the Lord in July, announced his call to preach in August, and was a student at Bob Jones University in September. As has already been noted by Norm Pollard's son, Norman Ray Jr., "When they turned their life over to the Lord back then, it was 100%!"

Ernie struggled with college. Although he was gifted in mathematics, reading was extremely difficult for him; and going from the tobacco fields of Eastern North Carolina to the opera-style music of BJU was a culture shock for the farm boy. After a year and a half of academic frustration, he switched to BJU's Institute for Christian Service from which he ultimately graduated. He would return to Eastern North Carolina and work as an electrician's helper during his school breaks. These breaks gave him additional opportunities to attend People's Baptist Church and to fellowship with Norm Pollard, Frank Smith, and other soul winners there. People's also hosted Sword of the Lord conferences which afforded him the opportunities to hear John R. Rice and some of the other preachers who traveled with Rice. Through the continual emphasis on revival and soul winning, God was preparing him well for his life ministry.

Ernie remembers one time when Dr. Rice was preaching that during the invitation Dr. Rice looked over his glasses directly at Ernie. Dr. Rice said from the pulpit, "Now, young man, you need to be saved; just come on down and settle it." Ernie was already saved, but out of respect for Dr. Rice's spiritual discernment, he began to search his heart. He was sure he was saved and everything was clear between him and God, but Dr. Rice just wouldn't drop it. Two or three more times as they continued singing, Dr. Rice looked directly at him and said again, "Come on now, you need to come down and be saved." Finally, after about four stanzas, the young man directly behind Ernie stepped out and went forward to be saved. Dr. Rice had not been looking at Ernie at all!

As graduation neared at BJU, Ernie Mills was reading Charles Sheldon's 1896 book entitled In His Steps. This novel describes a church making decisions by simply asking the question, "What would Jesus do?" As he prayed about what to do after graduation, it seemed that the answer for him was to do what no one had ever done for his alcoholic dad. He was to reach out to addicts and share the gospel and the love of Christ with them.

When he went into the office of Dr. Gilbert Stenholm (the same office from which Bill Wingard had been directed toward New Bern a few years earlier), Ernie discovered that God was once again working both ends of the problem. Ernie told Dr. Stenholm that he felt led to work in rescue missions. Dr. Stenholm just smiled and said that "by coincidence" Rev. Neil Wilcox had been in his office just the previous week. Rev. Wilcox had started a rescue mission in Winston-Salem after he had graduated from BJU only the year before. Wilcox was also a product of what God was doing in Eastern North Carolina, having come to BJU out of Grace Baptist Church in Kinston where the Eborns had been members. Now, Rev. Wilcox had returned to BJU to recruit help for the new mission he had started in Winston-Salem.

God worked out the details and Ernie agreed to go work with Brother Wilcox at the Winston-Salem Mission. Ernie Mills was ordained by People's Baptist in Greenville on June 7, 1968. It was four years to the day after he had gotten saved there. Then, he immediately went to work in Winston-Salem. Ernie's first assignment for the Rescue Mission was to gather all the clothes that students graduating from BJU had abandoned by dumping them into the universities' "mission barrels." He loaded them all into a U-Haul truck that Wilcox had rented and hauled them to the rescue mission location in Winston-Salem.

Ernie went to work and the Lord blessed as he learned the ins and outs of running a rescue mission. One unexpected blessing that came was that one evening as he was leading a church service an attractive young lady walked in as a chaperone of a group of teenagers who were going to help with the service (although Brother

Ernie prefers to jokingly say that she "staggered in with the clients"). He asked about her and whether she was dating anyone. The girl he asked said, "O yeah, she's dating my brother Junior." Ernie thought, "Well, that's the end of that." The service went on, and the group left. The attractive young lady, whose name was Gail Gerry, took a couple of her friends to McDonald's after the service. When she learned that Ernie had asked about her, Gail immediately insisted that her friend find a pay phone *right then*, and let Ernie know that she was NOT dating Junior. Junior only picked her up for church.

That meeting eventually led to Gail Gerrey becoming Mrs. Ernie Mills. She joined him at his work at the Winston-Salem Rescue Mission, and for 5 ½ years they continued learning, serving, and helping. Then, in 1973, they felt strongly that it was time for them to strike out on their own and open a similar Rescue Mission in Durham, North Carolina. It wasn't an easy decision. By that time, they had a 1 ½ year old son named Ernie, Jr. and they owned a 14-acre plot of land with a mobile home on it. Striking out on their own would be extremely risky. Financially, the timing was horrible. Prices rose at an annual rate of 6.8% over the first three quarters of 1973. Amid this inflation and the associated layoffs, it was no time to be asking people for money to start a new rescue mission. Yet, these same circumstances made the need for a mission greater than ever.

The start of the Durham Rescue Mission has already been well documented in a book entitled A Step of Faith by Andrea Higgins. It was released in 2006. But for those who have not read that account, we'll provide a short summary of how God used the nineteen-year-old young man that Norm Pollard had led to the Lord in the revival service in 1964.

Ernie and Gail sold their acreage and had their 10 x 55 mobile home towed to Durham. They hauled two 55-gallon drums of heating oil with them because they knew oil companies weren't accepting new customers due to the oil embargo in place at that time. They didn't know a soul in Durham. They spent the first year making the rounds to the churches looking for support. They didn't have a building to put a Rescue Mission in, and few donations came in.

The faith behind their step of faith was severely tested in 1974. Their second child, a girl whom they named Bethany, was born prematurely and with Highland Membrane Disease. For her first 72 hours, they didn't even know if she would survive. Thankfully she did survive, but she remained in the hospital for weeks; and Ernie and Gail had no medical insurance. Ernie was scheduled to speak at a conference. At Gail's insistence, he attended the conference even though Bethany was still in the hospital. God used a message from Psalm 145:3 which was preached by Pastor Bobby Thomas of Calvary Baptist Church in Greenville, North Carolina, to encourage him. Brother Bobby preached, *Great is the Lord, and greatly to be praised.* At this low point in his life, there was little praise left in Ernie Mills, but this passage reenforced what he knew in his heart. Circumstances hadn't changed the fact that *Great is the Lord!* and that indeed He is still *greatly to be praised.*

When the other preachers heard of Ernie's burden, they took up an offering to help with the medical bills. One retired pastor didn't have any money to give, so he gave his watch. God moved miraculously. Bethany was able to come home, and through the generosity of God's people the hospital bills were paid in full within three months. Thankfully, a few key supporters also slowly began to befriend the young couple and to finance their burden for a mission.

Ernie found a dilapidated old house at 1301 East Main Street in Durham. The homeless had already claimed it, breaking down the doors and knocking holes in the walls to drop their beer and wine bottles into (Ernie would later joke that most homes have fiberglass insulation in the walls, but their first mission house literally had glass for insulation in the walls). Ernie and Gail emptied their bank account of all but $100 for a down payment, and then sold bonds at a 7% interest rate to buy the property. But they had no money for repairs, and the building inspector promptly gave them a long list of requirements which had to be complied with in order to keep the building from being condemned.

Ernie and Gail were thrilled when the first client came to spend the night. However, they were heartbroken the next morning when he said, "I appreciate what you all are trying to do, but I've got to find some place warm." He left. Ernie hauled a load of the wine and beer bottles to the local dump. He despised the alcohol that had killed his father, and was angrily kicking the bottles from the bed of his truck when he looked up and saw a gas space heater sitting on top of the trash. It looked to be in almost new condition. He took it home and had a friend who worked at a gas company to inspect it to ensure it was safe to use. It was in perfect working condition.

An anonymous donor gave a brand new hot water heater, and another friend tutored Ernie in plumbing. With his help, Ernie ran new plumbing throughout the house. A real estate developer donated two 55-gallon drums of paint. One barrel was cream colored and the other was an avocado green that screamed 1970s. Mission residents helped them paint, sometimes painting around holes in the walls that they couldn't afford to repair yet.

The mission was responsible for feeding the men three meals a day, which provided its own challenges on their extremely limited income. A local grocery store donated a truck load of dented or damaged cans of food. However, to prevent any possibility of the food being sold, the store owner removed all the labels from the cans, making it impossible to plan meals. This made every meal a literal mystery meal. One of Ernie's solutions to the food problem was to ask neighbors if the mission could raise gardens on their property. Thankfully some agreed, and Ernie was able to put his farming background to good use.

From this humble beginning, God has wonderfully blessed the self-sacrificing faith of Ernie and Gail Mills and "***that revival continues until this day***" in unbelievable ways. Within a few years, God had miraculously provided a parsonage and allowed them to purchase the former Fuller Memorial Presbyterian Church building just one block away at 1201 East Main Street. A real estate developer also donated a rental house that he couldn't keep rented because the neighborhood was so bad. Later, they expanded to a second mission in neighboring Alamance County.

Although the ministry was expanding at an astonishing rate, Ernie and Gail never lost their vision of being able to always have one empty bed so that they never had to turn anyone away. They also had a growing burden for homeless women and children and began to seek ways to provide for them. And they were learning, constantly learning. In the beginning, they had assumed that what most homeless people needed was a job; however, as the homeless shelters began to be occupied more and more by drugs addicts instead of those with alcohol addictions, they recognized that helping the homeless get a job wasn't enough. All too often the jobs simply provided income to fuel the drug addictions.

In response, the Rescue Mission developed a program which they named the Victory Program after the wording of I Corinthians

15:57, *But thanks be to God, which giveth us the victory through our Lord Jesus Christ.* Those accepted into the Victory Program are allowed to stay for six months of rehabilitation before going out to find jobs. During this time clients attend classes four hours a day and then perform chores around the mission. This was yet another step of faith because it placed the full expense of the client's stay on the Mission, whereas before, the working men had contributed some of what they earned. But once again, God blessed faith. The Victory Program has resulted in numerous exciting testimonies of those who have been delivered from their addictions through the saving grace of God.

In 2002, God opened doors for the Durham Rescue Mission to minister to women and children in a way that was *exceeding abundantly above all* they had dared ask or think (see Ephesians 3:20). The 60,000 square foot, 130-room Durham Inn had become a haven for drug addicts and prostitutes and was under siege by neighbors and government officials who wanted it demolished. Ernie began to investigate the possibilities. The Inn owner agreed to finance $350,000 if they could raise a $400,000 down payment within 90 days. By the grace of God and the generosity of God's people, the $400,000 was in the bank within 57 days. This was all the more miraculous because this money was raised during the financial uncertainty following September 11, 2001.

The Durham Rescue Mission has grown to where they are now providing berthing for over 400 men, women, and children every night; and they are constantly expanding. But amid all the hustle and bustle of constant expansion, the concern for individual souls has never diminished. When Brother Mills was asked as a final question during our interview, "What is the greatest thing you've seen God do?" Ernie began to tell the story of Alex Winn. Alex had had a full scholarship to Duke University, but while there he became addicted to drugs. For ten years, he wandered, finally ending up at the Rescue Mission on a cold winter night in 2018. Alex rededicated his life to the Lord and graduated from the Rescue Mission's Victory Program. Incredibly, Duke University gave him another scholarship, and Alex has now graduated with two degrees, one in artificial intelligence related to medicine and one in neuroscience. He then continued his studies toward a master's degree.

Ernie and Gail's genuine love for the individuals at the Mission are reflected in his selection of this testimony as the greatest thing God has done. He doesn't think first of all the great financial miracles or the incredible favor God had given the mission with donors as the greatest thing God has done over the decades of mission work. Instead, he views the greatest thing that God has done as being the fact that God has turned around one life at a time. Although, Alex's testimony was the one most recently on his mind on the day of the interview, one gets the sense that you could have asked Ernie that question at any time over the past five decades and he would have started talking about an individual who had become *a new creature in Christ Jesus* (II Corinthians 5:17).

To an indescribable extent, the revival that resulted in a nineteen-year-old young man's salvation in 1964 ***continues until this day***. The Rescue Mission sponsors four major evangelistic outreaches each year. Between the individual clients who get saved at the mission and these outreaches, over 2,700 eternal souls were saved between 2017 and 2022. Many of them have also been delivered from addictions and abusive circumstances. Many of them are also now actively reaching others in their own ways and ministries.

But saving Ernie Mills was just one instance of what God was getting started in 1964. In New Bern, God was about to use a very routine event to pave the way for thousands more to be saved.

Chapter Seven
1964 World Wide New Testament Baptist Missions

It was time for a haircut, so the tall thirty-year-old pastor who was becoming affectionately known around New Bern as "Preacher Bill" went into Wilbur Hughes's barber shop. As he waited his turn in the chair, he picked up the February 29, 1964, edition of the *Saturday Evening Post* and began to read it. An article entitled "America's Neglected Colonial Paradise" caught his attention. It was an article on the U.S. Trust Territory of Micronesia that the U.S. had received responsibility for after World War II. Parts of Micronesia would later form The Federated States of Micronesia in 1979 and would finally gain independence in 1986, but in 1964 it was all still a much neglected U.S. Trust territory.

In the busyness of recuperating from World War II, America had adopted what the article referred to as a "Zoo theory" regarding

Micronesia. Americans chose to "leave the natives in primitive bliss." The reality was that there was little bliss in the results of this theory. The islands which had been relatively prosperous under Japanese rule prior to WWII were now in a pathetic state of decay. Fields could not be farmed because of unexploded ordnance that the U.S. was still in the process of slowly recovering. Sunken boats and even sunken tanks littered the waterways. Schools were being conducted in bombed out Japanese headquarter buildings. Drinking water was polluted and had caused illness and two deaths. Governmental responsibilities were neglected. One example of this neglect can be found in the administration of radio oversight. The FCC considered the Micronesian Trust radio stations foreign, and the Voice of America considered their stations domestic; so for two decades Micronesian radio fell in the gap between the FCC and Voice of America. During that time the Micronesian Islands received only the Communist transmissions from Radio Moscow and Radio Peking.

Pastor Wingard found one photograph in the *Saturday Evening Post* issue particularly riveting. The photographer had skillfully captured an image of a man with a bowl of water bathing the injured foot of a man clad only in a loin cloth. The injured man was sitting on a ledge while a half dozen other loincloth-clad men and boys looked on. God began to get hold of Preacher Bill's heart. Brother Wingard had been a Navy corpsman who was serving with the 1st Marine Division when he got saved at 21 years old. Mrs. Wingard was also a Registered Nurse. As he viewed the photograph, the thought came to him: "I could do that." As Preacher Bill would later describe what happened there, "God got ahold of my heart like He never had in my life before." After getting his haircut, he hurried across to the Palace motel and bought his own copy of that leap year edition of the *Saturday Evening Post*.

He devoured the magazine and learned more about Micronesia. In 1961, a 100-page report from a United Nations mission had been released. The mission had found "considerable dissatisfaction and discontent" among the 81,000 souls of the islands of Micronesia. The report was a public embarrassment to the Kennedy administration, and the wheels were set into motion to begin making changes before President Kennedy was assassinated in November, 1963. One important change that opened doors for God's program was that money was allocated to get radio stations back on the air.

The souls of Micronesia became somewhat of an obsession for Bill Wingard. He talked about it everywhere he went. He was already making tapes for a radio program which he called The Calvary Hour, so he wrote letters to some radio stations in Micronesia and asked them about the possibility of getting some air time out there. He explored every option with a burdened, breaking heart for the unsaved souls in Micronesia. His family would go to bed and he would get his copy of the magazine out and read it again. At times, he would sit and weep. The radio stations never responded. Nothing opened up. It seemed as if there was a wall of separation between his burden and Micronesia.

After some time, he volunteered to go as a missionary himself even though God was now greatly blessing the ministry at Calvary Baptist Church in New Bern and he didn't want to leave it. A family offered to raise funds to buy a sailing vessel so he could go and minister from it while it was docked at the various islands. The boat was to be named the April Dawn after their daughter who had died. But everything fell through. It became evident that it wasn't the Lord's will for Preacher Bill to leave Calvary Baptist Church and go to Micronesia, yet the burden never left him.

Months and years passed, but still nothing opened. He prayed about it constantly. Finally, in February, 1971, he felt impressed to write to the radio stations again. This time two stations responded. Preacher Bill sent some tapes to them and his sermons were broadcasted by WSZD on the island of Pohnpei, which is the main island of what is now the Federated States of Micronesia. The tapes were played by another station on the island of Yap as well.

An American school teacher named Charles Massey heard the broadcast in Pohnpei. He wrote to Bill Wingard saying, "We need this kind of preaching out here!" He included a gift of twenty dollars, but even more important than sending financial support and encouragement, Brother Massey was the means by which God connected Pastor Wingard with a Mokilese pastor named Isamo Welles (Mokilese indicates that he was from the small outlying atoll of Mokil, which had a population of less than 200). Brother Welles had been a drunken college student on Guam, but in February 1964, an American serviceman had led him to the Lord. By divine coincidence, that just happened to be the same month that Bill Wingard had stumbled across the *Saturday Evening Post* article. God had done a great work in both their hearts and lives over the intervening seven years. While Wingard was pastoring, struggling, and praying over Micronesia, the American serviceman had observed great potential in Isamo Welles, so he had helped get Brother Welles enrolled in Prairie Bible Institute in Alberta, Canada. Isamo Welles went from the tropical heat of Micronesia to Canada's often freezing temperatures, milked cows, and did what he had to do to work his way through Bible college.

Greatly burdened for his own people, he then returned to Pohnpei and began to evangelize, engaging in personal soul winning. So far as he knew, he was the only born-again Christian on the island; but by the grace of God, he was able to lead a few to Christ. One person who got saved was a lady named Esther. Esther was from a royal family on the island, and she soon became his wife.

He and Esther built a house and intentionally built the living room large enough to host church services so they could start a church. Soon, they had about ninety children attending their Sunday School (visualize ninety pairs of flip flops lined up outside their front door every Sunday morning)! However, no adults would attend the services. In Pastor Wingard's words, "The Congregational Church out there had power that would make Rome envious." Since, Micronesia was still a U.S. Trust Territory at that time, Brother Welles supported his growing family by serving as the U.S. Postmaster for the island.

Brother Welles and Pastor Wingard began to correspond often. Then in the same week, Pastor Wingard received two troubling letters, one from Pastor Welles and the other from Charles Massey. A group was planning to translate the liberal paraphrase "Good News for Modern Man" into the local language. Both men were greatly concerned about the effect this would have on their efforts to present the truth of the gospel. On Monday morning, Preacher Bill followed the example set by Hezekiah centuries before. He went into the new Calvary Baptist Church auditorium, which was still under construction at the time. There, he knelt, and spread the two letters before the Lord. As he prayed over those letters, he told the Lord that he would borrow the money if necessary, so that he could go help in Micronesia.

At the following Wednesday night church service, Preacher Bill shared his burden with the church family and asked them to join him in prayer for Micronesia. Many were burdened and effectual fervent prayer ascended into heaven. On Thursday morning a man who had just gotten saved, and who had also just recently retired, walked in and thrust his hand out to Pastor Wingard. He said simply: "Here, go make that trip," then he shoved a roll of $50 and $100 bills into Bill Wingard's hand. At that time, it cost $705 to fly round trip from Kinston, North Carolina to Pohnpei (the same flight costs approximately $3,500 today).

Preacher Bill began to prepare for a trip to the group of islands that he had not even known existed until seven years earlier. He would later admit that after all this time, when the reality that he was actually going hit him, it frightened him. Thankfully, God had a Barnabas to come alongside and be a help to him. Brother Jerry Gurganus, who at that time was a deacon at Calvary Baptist Church, came and told Preacher Bill that he felt led to go with him. While in the Air Force, Jerry had been stationed in Hawaii and had flown out from there to Guam, Okinawa, and other islands. These military experiences had given Brother Gurganus some familiarity with traveling in the Pacific, while Bill Wingard knew only what he had read.

Gurganus had been saved at Calvary Baptist Church in 1966 when Evangelist Jack Greene was preaching a revival there. By 1971 when this first trip to Micronesia was beginning to take shape, he was actively serving in the church while still working on board MCAS Cherry Point as a civilian. When Jerry found out that Pastor Wingard expected to be gone 3-4 weeks, he expressed his doubts. Due to the workload associated with Cherry Point's support of the war in Vietnam at the time, it was highly unlikely he'd be able to get more than two consecutive weeks off, with or without pay. They decided to use his leave request as a fleece to confirm whether he should go. When they learned that Jerry was applying for three weeks leave, his coworkers laughed at him. But Jerry submitted his leave request anyway, annotating on it that he wanted to go on a mission trip to Micronesia. He had the leave slip back in his hands in less than an hour and it was approved. It was one more confirmation that God was in all this, and He quickly provided the additional money needed to cover Jerry's expenses as well.

Brother Welles had requested that if they came to Pohnpei, they bring Bibles. Bearing Precious Seed publishing ministries in Ohio agreed to provide 1,000 New Testaments. That was a tremendous blessing, but it quickly dawned on Preacher Bill and Jerry that the Bibles totaled almost 500 pounds of additional luggage that they would have to get to Micronesia. Once again, they went to God in prayer; then they contacted the three airlines that they would be using to fly over. Continental Air Micronesia responded that they couldn't help, and one airline never responded. But Braniff Airlines graciously offered to ship the Bibles as far as Honolulu free of charge if they could get them from Ohio to Braniff's freight hub in Chicago. In Hawaii, they would be responsible for moving them from the arrival terminal to the departure terminal and then securing freight to Micronesia. Pastor Wingard and Brother Gurganus made the arrangements to get the Bibles to Chicago, and when the time came, they got on a plane themselves.

The pastor and his deacon landed in Hawaii unsure of how they were going to get the 1,000 New Testaments the additional 3,000 plus miles to Micronesia. Walking into the huge airport freight warehouse, they met the man who processed freight for Braniff Airlines. He was typing invoices as Pastor Wingard approached him. Gurganus hung back, praying silently. It turned out that this same man who processed the freight for Braniff Airlines also processed the freight for Continental Air Micronesia, which was the airline that would take them on that last leg of the trip. When he learned that their boxes contained Bibles, he stopped typing, and pulled their invoices from his typewriter. He said, "Man that's a rough part of the world where you're going." Next, he handed them some stickers and said "Here, take these stickers and put them on those boxes." The two Eastern North Carolina men were shocked to learn that those stickers meant that they had free freight straight to Pohnpei for the 500 pounds of New Testaments! Concerned that the man might get in trouble, Pastor Wingard said, "But back in the states they told us you were not able to do this." The freight manager just smiled and replied, "We do things different out here." He handed them his business card and said, "If you have anything else going that way, let me know."

But they still really had no idea of the scope of the miracle God had just performed. When they landed, they learned from the locals that freight was backed up both in Hawaii and Guam waiting to come into Pohnpei. People were waiting for weeks and months to receive shipments. But when they had touched down at the Pohnpei International Airport, a quarter of a ton of God's Word had touched down on the same plane with them and at no cost to them!

When they got to Pohnpei, Brother Welles suggested they begin a revival. They secured use of the Ohmine Elementary School building, announced on the radio that they would be having a revival with Brother Wingard preaching, and would be handing out free New Testaments. Thankfully many of the adults who had declined to come to the Welles' home for church services did choose to attend the services in the public school building. For some reason, Pastor Welles chose to have someone else serve as the interpreter. As Pastor Wingard would later describe it, "The first night was a flop, an absolute flop." Whether it was because of Brother Wingard's southern English or because the interpreter had an inadequate command of the English language is unknown, but the upshot of it was that the first night was an absolute fiasco.

English was a second language to most on the island, and for some it was not an understandable language at all; but in frustration, Brother Welles told Wingard, "Preacher, just preach like you do on the radio; just preach without an interpreter." Just months prior to his homegoing, Bill Wingard described the results with these words, "I did, and it was one of the few times I've seen the power of God fall, one of only two times. God came down. Scores of people got saved. The people that became the leaders of that church got saved. The back of that power was broken of people not coming to church, and that's how Calvary Baptist Church got started out there." God had wonderfully overcome the language and cultural barriers that existed.

Pastor Wingard had led his brother Stan to the Lord when Stan was a senior in high school. Stan also attended Bob Jones University; then he pastored churches in New York, Michigan, Georgia, and South Carolina. Ultimately Stan would settle into Community Baptist Church in Ayden, North Carolina, just forty miles from his brother in New Bern. Regarding this time of revival in Micronesia, Stan recalled, "He said it was like reliving the book of Acts for a period of time. People wanted them to preach as long as they would at night; and when they woke up the next morning, they were waiting for them to start preaching again." During those wonderful three weeks, the gospel seeds, which had been sown faithfully by

Isamo and Esther Welles and had been faithfully watered through the prayers of many, produced a wonderful harvest.

Prior to the departure of Pastor Wingard and Brother Gurganus, Calvary Baptist Church in New Bern had voted that they could ordain Isamo Welles if they deemed it appropriate to do so. They questioned him on Bible doctrine and found his Bible school training had prepared him well for the ministry. "He was solid as a rock." During that busy three weeks of holding revival, baptizing, discipling, and handing out Bibles, they were thrilled to also make time to baptize and ordain Isamo Welles. Brother Welles then delighted them by announcing that the church that was being started there on the island would also be named Calvary Baptist Church.

On the long flight home, God was still working. This time he was working in the heart of Jerry Gurganus. Brother Gurganus asked Pastor Wingard, "How can you tell if God's calling you to preach?" Preacher Bill was stretched out in the seat behind Gurganus, and he gave only a short, sleepy reply. "You'll know." At 30,000 feet over some nondescript pool of Pacific Ocean salt water in the dark of the night, Jerry Gurganus settled it. He prayed, "Lord, I'm here. I'm volunteering to preach; I feel like you're calling me."

As always, the response of the preacher's wife was critical. As Jerry was leaving for work on his first day back to Cherry Point, he told his wife, "The Lord's calling me to preach. If He calls you, let me know." That evening the dinner table was very, very quiet. Finally, his wife said, "I heard what you said this morning. God hasn't called me to preach. I don't believe God calls women to preach." Jerry agreed. Then she continued, "But what the Lord did do, He laid it on my heart that I follow you wherever you go; and I'll work with you wherever you go."

That was the green light of confirmation. By faith, Jerry quit his job, they sold their house, and went to Bob Jones University to prepare for ministry. He got a job setting up mobile homes near BJU. Times weren't easy for the family of five. At one point he seriously questioned whether God was in the whole thing or not. Another crew had set up a mobile home and had incorrectly connected the sewer lines. The family that moved in were all sick, and Jerry was assigned to reconnect the sewer lines properly. In the filth of that job, it just didn't seem possible that this was God's will for his life; but he stayed with it, and graduated from Bob Jones.

Back in Pohnpei, Brother Welles needed a building for his rapidly growing church. His living room was now too small. Land was very hard to come by, but his father donated a patch of land that had been used to grow taro. Taro is a plant that is similar in appearance to the decorative "elephant ears" plant, but taro is edible. Pastor Wingard found a 40 x 80 metal building in Rocky Mount, North Carolina. God quickly provided the money to purchase it, but once again they were faced with a huge logistics problem. How do you ship several tons worth of building material to a foreign island?

Once again in answer to prayer, God moved in numerous ways to provide. A trucker who had to "dead head" to the west coast to pick up a load agreed to haul the building that far. God provided the money for the shipping from the west coast to Micronesia. He provided a contact who arranged for stevedores to properly package the material and load it on a ship. By the grace of God, the building materials made it to the island, and the locals began preparing for its assembly. At that time, there were no hardware stores as we know them now on Pohnpei, and tools were scarce. In order to help with these matters, a group from Eastern North Carolina flew over to lend assistance and to provide the needed tools. When they arrived, they found that the natives had done a tremendous job of pouring the pad and preparing for assembly, especially considering how little they had to work with.

Due to the tropical heat, the Micronesians suggested that the Americans work in the morning and cease work in the heat of the afternoon; then the Micronesians would work in the evenings. Brother Chuck Lockwood, the brother-in-law of Clyde Eborn, wanted none of that and insisted on working through lunch. He hadn't flown all the way to Micronesia to put in anything less than a full day's work! So, while the other Americans went to lunch, Brother Lockwood continued working. As the others came out of a restaurant, they saw first responder lights flashing. They rushed to the job site and what they saw caused Bill Wingard's lengthy frame to shake with laughter decades later. The big former Marine aviator was dangling arms and legs out of a wheelbarrow as they rushed him to an ambulance. He had dehydrated and had passed out from heat stroke or heat exhaustion. They got some IVs into him, and thankfully he fully recovered with no lasting symptoms (no doubt, Pastor Wingard would not have been laughing if it had been otherwise). Each of the men who retold this story were gracious enough not to mention interservice rivalry, but it is quite likely that part of the reason they enjoyed telling the story so much was because Pastor Wingard had been a Navy Corpsman, Pastor Eborn was an Army veteran, and Jerry Gurganus had served in the Air Force. No doubt the big Marine was subjected to a lot of good-natured ribbing once it was confirmed that he was going to be okay.

The same evening that Lockwood passed out, the group of eight Americans each slept on air mattresses on the floor in Brother Welles' living room. Brother Lockwood still had an IV in him with the bag tied to a curtain rod. During the night, Pastor Wingard felt a strong urge to kneel at the foot of his bed and pray. Having been subjected to the same long trip, hard work, and tropical heat that had taken Lockwood down, he really didn't feel like it. However, the urge was overwhelming, so he finally crawled to the foot of his air mattress and began to pray. Suddenly, he sensed movement and saw something slithering across his pillow. He grabbed a jar of Noxzema that they had brought for sunburns and began beating on the critter. Pastor Eborn awoke and helped. They had killed what Pastor Wingard called a scorpion centipede. It had a stinger nearly as large as a grown man's little finger. If it had come across his face and he had instinctively swatted at it in his sleep, it likely would have stung him in one of his eyes. Only God knows what the result of such a sting would have been. But his obedience to God's call to prayer had spared him.

Jerry Gurganus had now completed his studies at BJU. While there he had searched for mission agencies servicing Micronesia and discovered that there were none. As a matter of fact, there was only one liberal Baptist church of any kind anywhere on the islands at that time. There were no Independent Baptists. One mission board offered to help from their offices in Australia, but that was the only avenue presented. Jerry came back to New Bern and met with Pastor Bill Wingard, Pastor Clyde Eborn, Pastor Russell Bell, and Pastor Robert Winstead. They decided to start a mission board and elected Pastor Wingard to set up the constitution and by-laws. They named it New Testament Baptist Missions.

By the time the four pastors met for a second time, they had discovered that another group out in the Midwest already owned that name. After much discussion, they settled on adding World Wide in front of New Testament Baptist Missions, and thus World

Wide New Testament Baptist Missions (WWNTBM) was begun. This is how the mission agency came to have such a long name.

Jerry Gurganus and his family went on deputation to raise the money to go to Micronesia. Again, the hand of God was seen very specifically while on deputation. Money was coming in steadily, but suddenly it stopped, as if a faucet had been turned off. They sought God but were uncertain as to why support had dried up. Then their son Jerry Jr. developed an earache. When they took him to the doctor it was determined that he needed tubes in his ears. The doctor told them that if he had flown prior to having the tubes inserted, it likely would have ruptured his ear drums. The tubes were inserted and support quickly began to come in again. In short order they were at 100%. Their delay was God's protection upon them.

They would ultimately be used of God to plant the first Independent Baptist Church on the portion of Micronesia known as the Marshall Islands. The Marshall Islands are made up of two groups of approximately parallel islands and atolls known as Ratak (sunrise) and Ralik (sunset). The atolls include the Pacific proving grounds which were used by the U.S. from 1946 to 1958 as a nuclear testing site. The most notable of these tests were those which occurred on Bikini Atoll, and then the test of the world's first hydrogen bomb on the Enewetak Atoll in 1952.

The Gurganus family settled on the Island of Majuro, which is the most populated area of the Marshall Islands. It is now the capital city of the Republic. They founded Majuro Independent Baptist Church which **continues until this day** under the leadership of a national pastor.

While there, Brother Gurganus had the privilege to speak at the constitutional convention when the Marshall Islands were in the process of seeking their independence from being a U.S. Trust Territory. The process began in 1965. The convention was considering instituting a state church structure which would recognize only the Congregational Church and Catholicism. Brother Gurganus and others spoke encouraging them to include Freedom of Religion instead. By the grace of God, when the constitution of the Republic of the Marshall Islands was finally adopted in May, 1979, Section One of their Bill of Rights stated:

> "Every person has the right to freedom of thought, conscience, and belief; to freedom of speech and of the press; to the free exercise of religion; to freedom of peaceful assembly and association; and to petition the government for a redress of grievances."

But before the missionaries ever got on the field, the Mission agency had to be registered with the government. On a Calvary Hour radio program, Pastor Wingard told of the trip to Saipan to officially register the mission that was in its infancy there. He was preaching from Zechariah 4:6 *...not by might, nor by power, but by My Spirit, saith the* LORD *of hosts* and gave this testimony:

> I marvel and I rejoice at how God blessed these men and others that I read about and I'm glad today that by God's marvelous grace there's some things that He has allowed me to witness, and He's allowed me to see. He has taught me that indeed it is not by might nor by power but by My Spirit saith the Lord of hosts.

> I'd like to share with you an incident that happened many years ago as we were going into Micronesia with missionary work. The Trust Territory headquarters at that time was in Saipan. Saipan was under control at that time of the U.S. government. We were supposed to have prior permission to go into Saipan to conduct government business. You

didn't have to have government permission to go in to be a tourist and so forth.

When we got to Saipan, we really found out that it was true that we needed government permission. I'm not going to embellish this. I'm not going to add to it, but I want to share with you an experience that I learned, that it is not by might nor by power but by My Spirit saith the Lord.

After landing in Saipan and attempting to go through immigration, we were asked what our business was in Saipan. When we told the man that we wanted to go to the Trust Territory headquarters to get material to register our mission, he wanted to see our special permission. We didn't have it.

I'm telling you dear friend, he exploded. I mean, he exploded. He began to holler at us and yell at us. He told us basically that we had broken the law and that he was going to put us on the next flight going out of Saipan. He was going to fine the airline for allowing us to come in without the proper papers. He couldn't say enough bad things about us.

What are you going to do? You're not going to jump up and say: well, I tell you I'm an American citizen and I'm not going to take this. No, he was the immigration officer there for the U.S. government. I'm telling you we were in a strait. We were in a hard time. Thank God for folks praying for us. In fact, I'm sure our team was in prayer at that time as well even if we couldn't get on our knees and pray at that time.

But you know what? In the midst of his bellicose statements, his hollering, his yelling at us, and his threatening us, he calmed down like Jesus calmed the waters of the sea. He said, "What is it that you fellows want?" We said, "We'd like to go to the Trust Territory headquarters and get the papers so that we can register our mission work here in the Pacific." You know what he did? He said, "I'll help you with that." This is the man that just threatened to throw us off the island and fine the airline! He said, "I'll help you with that."

He got off of work and went with us to the Trust Territory headquarters there in Saipan. He took us to every department we needed to go to, got all the papers for us that we needed, and we were complete. We had that completed in just a few hours, what would have taken days otherwise. Now, what do you attribute that to? It's not what, it's Who. Not by might nor by power but by My Spirit saith the Lord of hosts.

Ironically, after all the emphasis on Micronesia, the first missionary to be supported by World Wide New Testament Baptist Missions went to India. Joseph and Sarijoni Robert Garikimukkula had heard about WWNTBM through Tennessee Temple University and applied. They were accepted and began to minister in India first. However, the second family to receive support through WWNTBM was Isamo and Esther Welles, who were already ministering effectively in Pohnpei. They began to receive support in January 1972. After them, Jack and Jonnie Hunt signed on as the third missionary family with WWNTBM. The Hunts remained in America and supported missionary aviation (more on their ministry in chapter 11). Jerry and Eleanor Gurganus were the fourth family to sign on in March of 1974.

Others quickly followed with George Crompton signing on as deputation secretary, Roy Jernigan ministering to American Indians in Texas, and Dennis and Jean Jester also quickly joining the island ministry.

The bad experience with the tropical heat didn't deter Lockwood. In 1974 Chuck Lockwood and his wife Laura would become the eighth missionary family to sign on with World Wide NT Baptist Missions. They returned to Micronesia and served as missionaries; then after returning to America, Brother Lockwood continued serving the Lord as a pastor.

Brother Isamo Welles would go on to be respectfully referred to as "The Apostle Paul of Micronesia." Again, **to some extent, that revival continues until this day**. Today, there are seven Baptist Churches on the island of Pohnpei. Because some were started by American missionaries, Calvary Baptist makes no claim to be their "mother church." However, their startup was often assisted by Isamo Welles and Calvary Baptist Church. One missionary described Calvary Baptist's role in helping the others get started as a "big sister" role. Calvary Baptist Church itself continued to flourish under the leadership of William Joel, the "double brother-in-law" of Isamo Welles (they married each other's sisters). The Christian school which Calvary Baptist Church of Pohnpei hosts now has over 300 students, is highly respected, and doesn't have room to accommodate all the requests they have for children to be admitted.

Brother Welles's impact was not limited to Pohnpei. He reached out to other atolls and islands as well. For example, he helped plant a Calvary Baptist Church on the easternmost island of the Federated States of Micronesia, Kosrae. Because the language spoken on Pohnpei is similar to Pastor Wellis's native Mokilese, the differences were manageable. However, the natives of the island of Kosrae speak an entirely different language. Yet, Pastor Welles somehow overcame the language barriers and planted a church on Kosrae as well. Calvary Baptist Church of Kosrae also "***continues until this day***" under the leadership of a national pastor.

Pastor Welles also helped expand the radio work. In the mid-80s missionaries Dave and Ruth Ann Arthurs went to Pohnpei to help establish a radio station there through Calvary Baptist Church. It took over a decade to get all the approvals and actually get the station on the air. The church applied for and received a long term lease from the Pohnpei congress to use land and an existing radio tower that the American military had left after WWII. However, once the church cleared the land, squatters settled in. Although they had a legal right to the land, the church found that it was very difficult to get the squatters removed. At one point during the dispute, a group of loud, angry, machete-wielding locals approached the home where the Arthurs were staying. Brother Dave had his wife video tape him as he went out to talk with the group. He told her, "No matter what happens, just keep the tape rolling." He calmly and prayerfully explained to the angry men that the church had the legal rights to the property; and by the grace of God, the situation was deescalated. The church was finally able to build a fence around the tower. However, they never were able to gain full access to about 1 ½ acres of the property that the squatters continued to occupy.

The radio station helped to overcome some of the difficulties that the missionaries and Brother Welles had been struggling with. Most notably, the tight knit family culture of the islands created a situation where it was expected that children would continue in the church in which they had been reared. Any time a grown child chose to switch to the Baptist church, it created problems in the family. In order to discourage family members from leaving existing churches, misinformation and rumors began to circulate about the Baptists. The radio allowed people to hear for themselves what the Baptists actually believed and taught.

Missionary Gabriel Eiben and his family replaced Dave and Ruth Ann Arthurs when Brother Arthur's health failed to the point that he could no longer continue the work. In 2017, Missionary Eiben discovered an example of how that **to some extent, that revival continues until this day**. After two years of prayer, Brother Eiben partnered with a national pastor to make an evangelistic thrust to reach the people living on an atoll 27 miles from Pohnpei. Ten men boarded two 18' skiffs and struck out into the open water. As they departed Pohnpei, the atoll they were going to was not even visible. When they finally reached the atoll and preached, some of the locals received Christ. The team handed out solar-powered radios which were pre-tuned to the Calvary Baptist station on Pohnpei. One of the radios was given to a family of three who were the only residents on yet another tiny atoll. The father shared this testimony with them: "I have been listening to the Baptist radio for years, and what a tremendous difference it has made in my life." The radio signal from Pohnpei was literally reaching *unto the uttermost parts of the earth,* to a tiny atoll inhabited by only three humans!

The story of how God called the Eiben family to Pohnpei provides yet another example of how God works all the angles of a problem at the same time. Because the church where Gabe Eiben had been saved supported the Arthurs, Gabe was aware of their ministry. Then Dave Arthurs was diagnosed with leukemia. He came to America and spoke at the Bible college where Gabe Eiben was a student. He spoke about the need for someone to replace him. God began to burden Gabe's heart, although it was some time before he felt a definite call to go to Pohnpei. He had no background in radio. Previously, Dave Arthurs had also spoken at another church where a 19-year-old girl named Susan had surrendered to be a missionary. It was the one and only time Dave Arthurs ever preached at that particular church; but in 2002 that girl became Mrs. Gabriel Eiben. When Gabe called his pastor at the Calvary Baptist Church of Smithfield, Virginia, to let him know that he had surrendered to the call to Pohnpei to replace Dave Arthurs, Pastor Dan Gray told him: "Gabe, you don't know this; but when we started this church, we felt strongly that we should support missions. Dave and Ruth Ann Arthurs were the first missionaries we took on for support." And God added one more piece as He assembled that puzzle. Not only did God use Dave Arthurs at each of these key decision times; but during the years while all this was developing, Susan Eiben found her employment at a Christian radio station. She thus gained valuable experience in Christian radio. Their sending church pastor summarized all this by saying that "God had uniquely equipped" them for their very specific ministry.

To a wonderful degree, the revival that resulted in World Wide NT Baptist Missions being started **continues until this day.** World Wide has supported over 300 missionary families since its inception. A few accounts have been given here of churches started, souls saved, and miraculous workings of our Almighty and Omnipresent Lord. Only eternity will fully reveal all that God did when a preacher who needed a haircut read a *Saturday Evening Post* article.

But God wasn't limiting his work to barbershops and Micronesian atolls. Back in Eastern North Carolina, He reached into the university crowd.

Chapter Eight
1965 Bud Calvert Saved

The fledgling People's Bible Church in Greenville, North Carolina, which would later be known as People's Baptist, was only four years old. Norm Pollard and other charter members were serving faithfully, soulwinning, and looking for the Lord to come. The church now had a small building and was under the leadership of a fireball preacher by the name of Jack Mosher.

At East Carolina University, a young student who went by the name of "Bud" was all too heavily involved in the party lifestyle of the campus. Bud was the son of a service station owner and a praying Christian mother back in Virginia; but despite her best prayer efforts, Bud had dropped out of high school when he was 16, enlisted in the Army to become a paratrooper at 17, and was far from the Lord now as a 21-year-old student at ECU.

But God was at work. After a couple quarters at ECU, Bud went back home during the summer break, and while there he attended a singles' camp which was hosted by the church his mother was attending in Arlington, Virginia. The camp was actually held in Maryland. His mother's church was "a somewhat dead Independent Baptist Church." He would learn later that the pastor, though a good and Godly man, was a five-point Calvinist. There was no emphasis at all on soul winning and no public invitations to be saved.

Yet, at that camp, Bud observed a Christianity that was real. It wasn't so much the message that the evangelist preached that reached him; but as he sat around the campfire that evening, he heard his peers stand one after another and give their testimonies. There was a sincerity to it that registered; and there around the campfire, Bud's knowledge of Christ transferred from his head to his heart. He already knew about Christ and His sacrificial death on the cross for our sins, His burial, and His resurrection, and he had never questioned the reality of that; but he also had never applied the atoning work of Christ to his own sins. Romans 10:9-10 occurred in his life that night: *That if thou shalt confess with thy mouth the Lord Jesus, and shalt **believe in thine heart** that God hath raised Him from the dead, thou shalt be saved. For **with the heart** man believeth unto righteousness, and with the mouth confession is made unto salvation.*

Again, due to the Calvinistic influence at work in the camp, there was no invitation, no one took a Bible and walked Bud through the Romans Road, no one lined him up for discipleship classes. But God wonderfully changed him that evening as he placed his faith fully in Christ and Christ alone. Bud did the last of his smoking, drinking, and cussing on June 3rd. On June 4, 1965, he became a new creature in Christ Jesus.

The piano player at the single adult group was an attractive young Christian named Mary. She caught Bud's attention right away, first with her skills on the piano, but then quickly afterwards in other ways. Soon she and Bud were engaged. Mary worked in Washington, D.C. By yet another wonderfully divine coincidence, Mary "happened" to make friends with a coworker who was also engaged to a student at the college 275 miles to the south of Washington D.C. Her coworker's fiancée was saved and was attending People's Bible Church in Greenville, North Carolina. The co-worker's fiancée sought Bud out and invited him to attend services at People's.

There, Bud met Pastor Jack Mosher and fervent soul winners like Dave Woodard and Norm Pollard. Bud had never seen a preacher like Jack Mosher in action in a pulpit before. He was a fireball; "when he preached you could see the blood vessels in his brow." Norm Pollard also made a big impression. Bud would later say, "He was just always, there... had an infectious smile... always [saying], let's go soulwinning. ...that encouraged me, and I thought this is what the Christian life is all about. It is telling other people about the Lord and seeing them get saved as well. Norm just exemplified that testimony... he was the number one soulwinner there in the church.... he was the epitome of *stedfast, unmoveable, always abounding in the work of the Lord.*"

The church had a Thursday night visitation program that they kept talking about. After a while, Bud showed up and went out on soulwinning visitation for the first time. Dave Woodard was the first one to take Bud with him. The next Thursday he came back, and this time he was assigned to go out with Norm Pollard. Norm gave him a copy of John R. Rice's book <u>Golden Path to Successful Personal Soul Winning</u>; and through the influence of

Pastor Mosher, Dave Woodard, Norm Pollard, John Rice, and others, a soul winner's fire was lit in the young man's heart.

Soon, Bud was out soulwinning on his own. He ordered 2,000 copies of the God's Simple Plan of Salvation tract which had been written by Ford Porter back in 1933. Bud and the friend who had invited him to People's handed out all 2,000 copies of the tracts on the campus of East Carolina University in one day.

At this point Bud got a taste of the religious liberalism on campus. Pastor Mosher was going to teach a weeklong class on soulwinning. The pulpit was set up like a living room, with a couch, a TV, and a door. Excited, Bud went to the Baptist Student Union area on campus to invite others. He was sure he would get a car load, but not a single student agreed to come. Instead, one female student who happened to be a Lutheran, invited him to come meet her pastor. When he got to the pastor's home, the first thing the pastor did was to offer him a cigarette. After discussing this event with Pastor Mosher, Bud came to understand that even religious leaders have sometimes never been born again.

But Bud *had* been born again, and he wanted to serve God. At a missions conference at People's, he felt the call to go in the ministry. He answered the call. Pastor Mosher was a Bob Jones graduate and he advised Bud to leave ECU and transfer to BJU, which Bud did.

He and Mary had gotten married by then, and together they moved from Greenville, North Carolina to Greenville, South Carolina. They had a son while there, and Bud Calvert began to feel led to start a church back in his hometown of Fairfax, Virginia.

But he knew nothing about starting a church. Church planting had not been taught in his undergraduate program. After he had earned his degree at BJU, he took an ensemble on the road to represent the college because BJU had offered to pay for a year's worth of graduate school if he would be responsible for the ensemble. Bud assumed that church planting would be taught at the graduate level.

While the ensemble was on the road and singing at a church camp, Bud met Grant Rice. Rice was a church planter who started twelve churches and actively crisscrossed the nation helping church planters. When the ensemble was scheduled to go to Rice's home church in Chicago, Bud arranged to meet with him.

Rice asked, "What are you planning to do, when you get finished?"

Calvert: "Well I want to start a church."

Rice: "Well, what are you doing in grad school?"

Calvert: "They didn't teach me how to start a church, so I figured you'd learn that while you were in grad school."

Rice: "Aw, I can teach you how to start a church."

For an hour and a half after a church service in Chicago in the summer of 1970, Calvert plowed Rice with questions about starting a church. Then, with youthful confidence that the ninety-minute session was sufficient to replace graduate work, Bud Calvert canceled grad school and moved back to Fairfax, Virginia, with his wife and son.

The Calvert family rented a second floor apartment in Fairfax; and Fairfax Baptist Temple was birthed in that apartment,. The church grew steadily; but like Pastor Wingard in New Bern who had a vision for missions, God had given Pastor Calvert a vision for something greater than just starting and pastoring one church, although that in itself is a major accomplishment. In addition to the care of his church, Pastor Calvert's burden was for Fairfax Baptist Temple to help start other churches.

In 1977, Pastor Calvert felt a deep burden for black America. This passion resulted in his going to a parking lot in Washington D.C., and preaching from a parking lot near the Washington Redskin's football stadium for ten days. He continued working with the group who came, and over forty people were saved. Thirty-three followed the Lord in believer's baptism, and Northeast Baptist Temple was started. A local man opened his row house to the church startup. After about ten months, Brother Calvert turned the work over to a black preacher who had just graduated from college. This brief interlude of pastoring two churches at one time would be the only time that Bud Calvert would ever pastor any church besides Fairfax Baptist Temple.

God quickly built upon the experience of starting Fairfax Baptist Temple and Northeast Baptist Temple. A Bible Institute was started in Fairfax, and God began to call young men into the ministry. Soon, church planters from Fairfax Baptist Temple were planting churches in Puerto Rico, the Philippines, and another in the D.C. area. The Calvert's son Troy started a Spanish church and pastored it for 17 years using the Fairfax Baptist Temple facilities.

After retiring, Bud Calvert wrote a book entitled <u>God's Passion - A Manual on Church Planting for World Evangelism</u> which was published by Striving Together Publications in 2010. In the book 34 men are named who all were sent out by Fairfax Baptist Temple to start churches. Many of these church plants have also helped to start other churches. The number of churches planted either directly or indirectly through the ministries of Fairfax Baptist Temple totals over 100.

When asked, "What is the greatest thing you've seen God do in your lifetime?" Brother Calvert responded, "For us, just the fact that so many men in our church were called into the ministry.... In Fairfax, it's an expensive area, business people, educated people, a lot of that. I think it was kind of unusual, just a lot of people that have been used by the Lord, and that God called, and we were able to send out... some giving up jobs... some of them were younger.... We've got fellows all over the place now that have gone out and started churches. That's a big encouragement to us now...."

The "*revival continues until this day*" as can be seen by the fact that God used the brief time that Bud Calvert spent in Eastern North Carolina to ignite a fire that has already blossomed to at least 100 church plants. At the same time God was working in the heart of another one of Eastern North Carolina's native sons.

Chapter Nine

1967 Emmanuel Baptist of Swansboro Started

Before we get to 1967, let's back up to 1959 to see the salvation of the man who would eventually start the second Independent Baptist Church in Carteret County, North Carolina. In 1959 God was still using Norm Pollard in a great way at DuPont in Kinston, but by no means was God's power limited to Kinston. In the little community of Mill Creek where Robert Joyner would later pastor briefly, God was working. In the fall of 1959, a young man then known as Rusty and his wife of three years attended the Sunday services at Bayview Baptist Church, where R.E. Reece was serving as pastor.

God got hold of Rusty's heart, and he went forward to be saved. The pastor had him to read Romans 10:13 repeatedly: *For whosoever shall call upon the name of the Lord shall be saved.* Once the simple reality of this wonderful verse sank in, Rusty confessed Jesus Christ as his Lord and Saviour.

His young wife Mamie had gone forward with him, and they both got baptized in the Newport River at 3:00 p.m. that same day. Someone gave Rusty a Gideon New Testament. As a newborn babe, he had an appetite for the milk of the Word; and he just about devoured that New Testament between that Sunday afternoon and the next church service, which for them was the Thursday night prayer meeting. It was the custom at Bayview Baptist Church to go around the room giving testimonies on Thursday nights. The 19-year-old was bold and rowdy when running the roads, but public speaking wasn't something that he wanted anything to do with. After he had gotten saved, Pastor Reece had stood him in front of the church and asked, "What do you want to tell these people?" Rusty had answered, "Well, I just accepted the Lord as my Saviour. Pray for me." At that point in his life, that was the most he had ever said in front of a crowd.

But, less than a week later on that Thursday evening as testimonies were being given in the midweek service, Rusty could sense that something was different. People were standing and testifying in turn in an uncoordinated wave. As the wave neared him, he did not feel the fear of public speaking that he had experienced in the past. When it felt like it was his turn, instead of just standing at his pew to give a testimony, he walked forward and preached for about 15 minutes. He did the same thing each of the following Thursday nights. On that third Thursday night, after having been saved less than a month, Russell Bell announced to the church that he felt like God was calling him to preach.

Pastor Reece was not able to attend the Thursday night service when Rusty announced his call to preach. Someone in the church quickly made sure the pastor knew about it; and on that next Sunday, Pastor Reece gave Rusty a date and said, "Be ready." Now, the fear returned. What had he gotten himself into?

The date came for him to preach his first official sermon. As he took to the pulpit, he asked Pastor Reece: "If I get up there and can't say anything, will you finish it for me? The pastor graciously agreed to do so, and the young Mill Creek boy stepped into the pulpit. Tears streamed down his face, and by the grace of God he preached his first full sermon.

Eugene and Francis Lilly were members of the church, and they took the two young converts under their wing much as Neil and Verline Glenn had accepted the responsibility for Bill and Arlie Wingard as their discipleship charge in California. In Mill Creek the Lilly family opened their home and their hearts to Russell and Mamie and began discipling them. They would wisely present a scripture and then instead of lecturing on it, they would ask: "What do you think God is saying?" As the discussions followed, they would use scripture to explain scripture. Russell quickly became well grounded in the Word of God.

Prior to his salvation, Russell had been working at a shirt factory, but had quit after a dispute with a coworker. Now that he was saved, he visited a local church and talked to a lady who helped him get his job back. His old boss said to him, "I hear you got religion." Bell said: "No, I got salvation." His boss, who was a Jew, skeptically responded: "We'll see."

Once again, God proved that being born again does indeed make a new creature out of the soul who got saved. When the young preacher went back to the bar to pay his tab, he told the owner, "This is the last money you'll be getting from me." The bar owner scoffed and pointed to a regular sitting at the bar. He said, "He's a deacon at the Baptist church here in town; you'll be back." But unlike the deacon of the liberal church, Russell Bell was a new creature in Christ Jesus, and old things were passed away. He never went back to the bar.

He gave up his alcohol instantly, but God had to work on his tobacco habit. About a year after he had gotten saved, he attempted to witness to a lady named Mrs. Arnold. She helped his testimony tremendously when she told him to get his own life right first. When he asked, "What do you mean?" She pointed at the pipe in his shirt pocket. He asked, "You mean this pipe is going to keep me from telling you about Jesus?" She responded "No. But it's going to keep me from listening!" He quit smoking.

As God had done at DuPont, God once again used connections at a secular workplace to pave the way for the work of His kingdom. The practice of businesses opening their doors to preachers that was seen in New Bern had found its way to the shirt factory where Russell Bell was working as well. Each Wednesday, a preacher from the ministerial association would come in, and the shirt factory would shut down. Preachers were allowed about twenty minutes to speak to nearly 200 workers. This was all at company expense; the workers were still on the clock. One Wednesday, Bell was working in the warehouse when he got a call from the front office asking if he could come to the production area and preach. The scheduled preacher had not been able to make it.

Russell jumped at the opportunity and God used the occasion. The factory janitor heard him and liked what he heard. The janitor also knew a deacon from nearby Peletier Baptist Church and knew they needed a pastor. Connections were made, and at 24 years old,

Russell Bell found himself pastoring the little Southern Baptist Church at Peletier, North Carolina.

There were only nineteen members when he first began at Peletier in 1964; but after a little while of getting established, God began to bless in wonderful ways. By 1967, the church had exploded to 273 members. Many "hard people" were getting saved. In Bell's words, "There was a time when conviction ran in a community, and the community couldn't rest. It was (God's) own choosing. There wasn't anything we were doing that was unusual. There was a spirit of prayer. There was a hunger."

One example of how God was moving then and how "***to some extent, that revival continues until this day***" is visible through the testimony of a young couple named Arnold and Shirley Futrell. They visited Peletier Baptist Church on a Sunday morning when there were about 250 people present. As Pastor Bell preached, it seemed as if the Lord drew a circle around them. The thought came to him, "They'll never walk an aisle, you've got to go see them." On the next visitation night, he went to talk to them one on one.

When Pastor Bell arrived at the Futrell's home, Arnold was raking pine straw. The preacher offered to leave and come back later, but Arnold insisted they come in, but with one condition. There was a television program that the Futrell family liked and that they had been waiting to watch. They invited him to watch it with them and promised that they'd turn the TV off and talk after the show was over. They were true to their word. As soon as the ½ hour program was over, they instructed their son to turn the TV off, and Arnold said, "Preacher, I've got some things I want to ask you." Brother Bell, who'd already been waiting through the TV show, suggested: "Well, what about if I talk to you first, and then after that ask me your questions?" They agreed, and Pastor Bell presented the gospel to them. All three - father, mother, and son - got saved. After they had received Christ as their Lord and Saviour, Brother Bell asked, "Well, what about your questions? Arnold Futrell responded, "Don't have any." Their questions and doubts had been erased at the moment of salvation!

The Futrell family grew in the Lord, and Arnold surrendered to preach in 1968. Pastor Bill Wingard helped get him enrolled at Bob Jones in '69. After schooling, they joined the World Wide NT Baptist Missions team, raised their support, and arrived on Pohnpei on Dec. 31, 1973. They established Truth Independent Baptist Church there while Chuck and Laura Lockwood worked on another part of the island. The Futrells eventually left Truth Independent Baptist in the hands of a national pastor and returned home on furlough. They later returned and spent an additional thirteen years on the island of Yap where they were used by God to also establish Yap Baptist Church.

Although great things were happening at Peletier Baptist Church, God was sowing the seeds of change. Russell Bell had attended a revival at Grace Baptist Church in Morehead City. Pastor Eborn had invited Ernie Robertson to preach. Robertson had been Eborn's pastor at Grace Baptist Church in Kinston when Clyde had first gotten saved. But, during the revival Robertson had a death in the family and had to leave. Clyde Eborn then asked his friend Bill Wingard to come down from New Bern to fill in. Wingard was still in his first year at Calvary Baptist and was in the middle of the early turbulence. His sermon was, "The Little Maid and Naaman's Leprosy." It was a message that Bell never forgot. At that time Grace Baptist Church was still renting the small one-room building from the oil company, and it was hot inside. So, after the service they all stepped outside, and there in the parking lot a lifelong friendship was struck between the two young Independent Baptist preachers and the young Southern Baptist preacher.

Bell continued to pastor at the Southern Baptist Church but fellowshipped with the Independent Baptists. They would fellowship with him, but would never invite him to preach. He was learning more about why they were Independent and about the Biblical doctrines of separation. Pastors Wingard and Eborn were his mentors. They never said anything negative about the Southern Baptist Convention; they just preached Jesus. As Brother Bell would later remember it, "They weren't trying to identify counterfeit by knowing counterfeit; (but) by knowing the real thing, they were exposing it."

But Russell Bell, like many others, was becoming more and more troubled by what he was seeing in the Southern Baptist Convention. He would attend the SBC preachers' fellowship once a month on Mondays. Some of the preachers were very vocal in the praise of the Presbyterians and others who were canceling their midweek and Sunday evening services. Bell would leave the "fellowship" meetings deeply troubled. Their words and attitudes grated at his spirit. He longed to see God starting something. He had no desire to join others in rejoicing when the work of God was slowing down or stopping.

The final straw for Russell Bell came when Billy Graham accepted the Doctor of Humanitarianism Degree from the Catholic college at Belmont Abbey. Graham was not the president of the Southern Baptist Convention (SBC) at that time, H. Franklin Paschall was. Yet, Graham was arguably the most recognized name in the convention, and therefore his positions were viewed by some as representing the position of the SBC. In his acceptance speech, Graham called the gathering "a time when Protestants and Catholics could meet together and greet each other as brothers..." He went on to minimalize the doctrinal differences between the Catholics and the Baptists. There were many issues in the SBC at that time including a debate over the authority of the scriptures, but this endorsement of Catholicism was the final straw for Russell Bell. He knew it was time to pull out of the Southern Baptist Convention.

As he debated about how to leave, he considered trying to persuade the church to become Independent. Someone told him that the deed to the church property included a clause which said that if the church ever ceased to be a Southern Baptist Church, the property was to revert to the family who had donated it. Bell never saw the deed, but decided to resign rather than to drag the people of the church, whom he dearly loved, through any such turmoil.

When Pastor Bell left, a few people who shared his convictions left also. The first Wednesday night afterward they met in nearby Swansboro in the home of a man named Cap Wagner. Wagner worked on board the base at Cherry Point as a civilian and was active in the Navigators Bible study program. Navigators was strong in emphasizing scripture memorization, and this connection through Wagner helped Bell tremendously in his spiritual growth.

The small group moved to another man's home, then eventually found a house nearby that they could use as a church building. Whoever had lived in the house before had lived the sad life that results from the abuse of alcohol. Like Ernie and Gail Mills in Durham, the church folks had to remove beer and wine bottles and repair the damage done by the intoxicated. The floors were so nasty they had to be scraped before they could be scrubbed. Eventually, the place was made appropriate for church services and the small group began to grow under Bell's Spirit-filled preaching. The house quickly became too small. In 1967 Emmanuel Baptist

Church of Swansboro was officially started. It was the second Independent Baptist Church in Carteret County. Only Grace Baptist of Morehead City had been started earlier by Brother Bell's friend Clyde Eborn.

They found a piece of property for sale nearby, but the property was landlocked. At that time, North Carolina law did not require any adjoining property owner to give them access to their land. By faith, they bought the property anyway, and later God did provide them with a right of way to the property they had purchased.

They went to work building a cinder block building, and God continued blessing. People were getting saved; and the little group, which had started out with about thirty people, was growing. God's Spirit was working. One day as they were laying block, a lady pulled up and honked the horn. She called for Pastor Bell. He climbed down from the scaffold and went to talk to her. She said, "I've been watching you people... I want what you got." Pastor Bell told her, "You sure can have it. But it only comes with Jesus." She retorted, "I want nothing to do with that." "That's the only way it comes, ma'am. It comes Jesus wrapped. He is the only Way." Unfortunately, like the rich young ruler in Matthew 19:22, she ...*went away sorrowful.*

In spite of the busyness associated with the growth at Emmanuel Baptist Church in Swansboro, Pastor Bell made time to help other ministries also. There was tremendous fellowship and cooperation among the Independent Baptist preachers. Harold Sightler once told Bill Wingard that he didn't know of anywhere in America where the preachers got along any better than they did in Eastern North Carolina.

Pastor Alex Bledsoe was in the process of erecting a metal building for Maranatha Baptist Church of Alliance, North Carolina.

The tiny town of Alliance (population 809 in 2019) was two counties away, approximately sixty miles from Emmanuel Baptist in Swansboro, but Russell Bell made the trip numerous times to help. He helped with the physical construction of the building, including trying his hand at welding for the first time in his life. Brother Bell's construction skills were a blessing to several churches. He would go on to lead four of the six churches he would pastor in major building programs.

One day as they were working in Alliance, he felt an extremely strong impression to "go home." He really didn't want to. Like Brother Lockwood in Pohnpei, he wanted to stay and put in a full day's work. It wasn't worth the effort to make the drive and only work part of a day. But the impression was very strong, and it wouldn't leave him. Finally, he told Pastor Bledsoe about it, apologized for ducking out early, and started toward home.

As Pastor Bell was traveling back toward Swansboro, he picked up a sailor who was hitchhiking near New Bern. The sailor was traveling south on Highway 17 toward Jacksonville. Brother Bell witnessed to him for about ½ hour as they traveled down Highway 17; but when they got to Maysville, he had to drop the hitchhiker off so that he could take route 58 east and continue toward Swansboro.

As Pastor Bell turned on to Highway 58, he had not gone a quarter mile before a thought seemed to scream in his mind, "WHAT ARE YOU DOING? Go back, and get that boy; that is why you are here!" Bell looked at the gas gauge. He was driving a '66 Volkswagen Beetle which got great gas mileage, but he barely had enough gas to make it home. There was no way he could add the additional 32 mile round trip to Jacksonville and still get home, and he didn't have any money with him. Even VW bugs don't go far on the memories of gas in their tanks. But the thought wouldn't leave him. "Go back!"

Bell spun the little VW around and picked up the sailor again. They talked some more. It turned out the sailor was going home to Georgia on leave, then would return to Norfolk and go to sea from there. Pastor Bell continued witnessing to him; and when they got to Jacksonville, they got out of the car and continued their conversation. Finally, there under a street light near the bus station in Jacksonville, North Carolina, the young sailor prayed and asked Christ to be his Saviour.

The sailor told Brother Bell, "When I get off this maneuver, I'd like to come to your church and tell the people what happened to me." They parted, and Brother Bell instantly experienced complete peace. He no longer felt the overwhelming impulse to "go home." He knew he had accomplished the task for which the Holy Spirit had been guiding him home. Miraculously, he drove into Swansboro with gas still in the tank.

But the story doesn't end there. The sailor had disclosed that he was assigned to a nuclear submarine called the *U.S.S. Scorpion*. Shortly after the sailor got saved, on May 22, 1968, the *U.S.S. Scorpion's* name was added to a list of three other mysterious submarine disappearances that occurred in 1968. It was October of 1968 before the Navy succeeded in locating the remains of the Scorpion. She was found about 400 miles southwest of the Azores in about 9800 feet of water. She was lost with all 99 hands on board. The other submarines lost that same year were the Israeli INS *Dakar*, the French submarine *Minerve*, and the Soviet submarine *K-129*. The cause of the loss of the Scorpion and the other submarines is still much debated.

Russell Bell never forgot the feeling that came over him when he first saw on the news that the Scorpion had disappeared. Thank God he had listened to that still small voice that told him to "go home" on a day when he was badly needed on the church construction project in Alliance. Like Phillip, who left a revival in Samaria to go witness to one Ethiopian eunuch, he had gone. At least one sailor is in heaven as a result. Only God knows whether that sailor had the opportunity to lead any of his shipmates to the Lord before that fateful Wednesday of May 22, 1968.

Emmanuel Baptist Church of Swansboro was continuing to grow. They had over 120 members, but Russell Bell was feeling a stirring in his soul again. This time, he was feeling the need to get more education. Although he was well versed in the Bible and God had already greatly used him in two churches, he felt the desire to learn more. He decided to go to Bob Jones University, the school from which his friend Bill Wingard had graduated.

Evangelist Ron Comfort came to Emmanuel Baptist Church for a revival. Comfort would go on to start Ambassador Bible College later in 1989, but this was twenty years before that time. God really blessed and they had "a real meeting." But amidst all the blessings, Bell's mind was on his upcoming resignation. He just didn't feel like he could handle standing before another congregation that he had come to love and resign alone. He had led many of them to the Lord. With Ron Comfort's permission and support, he stood before his church and resigned on the last night of the revival. He and his family were off to BJU.

Through a chain of events, God opened doors for Brother Bell to pastor in Keeseville, NY, instead of attending BJU at that time. He pastored in NY from 1970-1973. It was while he was pastoring there in New York that he partnered with Bill Wingard,

Clyde Eborn, and Robert Winstead to found World Wide New Testament Baptist Missions.

From New York, Russell Bell went on to be an Associate Pastor for Brother Ernie Robertson, who by then had moved from Kinston, North Carolina, to Easley, South Carolina. Here, under Ernie Robertson's guidance, he had the privilege of getting some of the mentoring and training which he had desired when he resigned from Emmanuel Baptist to go to BJU. He went on to start Landmark Baptist Church of Easley. While in South Carolina, he also managed to squeeze in some classes at BJU. He then ended the pastoring portion of his ministry with twenty years at Calvary Baptist Church in Henderson, North Carolina. Each church he pastored grew under his leadership. All grew numerically, plus he led four of the six churches through major building programs as was mentioned previously.

After resigning from Calvary Baptist Church in Henderson, Brother Bell "retired" to a life of evangelism and serving as a representative for WWNTBM. Despite major health issues and age, he continued to travel and to be a tremendous blessing and encouragement to many churches along the eastern seaboard.

Norm Pollard led Clyde Eborn to the Lord at DuPont. Eborn encouraged and befriended a "ready to resign" Pastor Bill Wingard in New Bern. Eborn and Wingard in turn befriended and influenced a young Southern Baptist preacher named Russell Bell. What would God do next?

Chapter Ten
1972 Starting Christian Schools

While God was doing great things in the churches in the 60s and early 70s, the world around them was getting crazier and more ungodly. The hippie movement, Vietnam, the "sex, drugs, and rock and roll" culture, and Supreme Court decisions were all taking their toll on attitudes toward God and the Bible. Parents were becoming more and more concerned about what their children were being exposed to in the public schools. These concerns gave rise to a large transfer of students from the public schools to private schools.

North Carolina, like most of Colonial America, already had a rich history in Christian schools. Even prior to the American Revolution, an academy was organized in Wilmington. In New Bern, money had been raised to start a school, but the money was "borrowed" by Governor Tryon to build his palace. Other communities also saw schools started.

There were multiple motivations behind the great wave of interest in private Christian schools in the 70s. Some point to the fact that the South led the nation in the retreat from public schools and claim that racism was the reason. There was certainly an element of truth in this accusation as America struggled with forced busing as a result of the 1954 Brown v. Topeka Board of Education Supreme Court decision. This decision declared segregated schools to be unconstitutional but didn't specify methods to end segregation. Little was done, until the Court followed with another ruling in 1955 ordering the school systems to "desegregate with all speed." This decision led to forced busing, which was not well received at all.

Pastor Eborn remembered some of the mood of America, or at least the mood of the South, during those early days. The church buses from Grace Baptist were picking up children on a Saturday for a youth meeting. Two black boys wanted to ride the bus to the event. The bus captain stopped and found a phone to call back to the church so he could ask Pastor Eborn what to do. Eborn enthusiastically replied, "Bring them on!" The bus captain did, but then some church members left the church over it. Later, a well-known evangelist who was preaching at another church in the area told Eborn that he was making a mistake by integrating Grace Baptist church (this evangelist is not named anywhere in this book). That evangelist went to heaven years ago. No doubt, he is now aware that heaven is fully integrated.

But the reality is that although racism may have been a factor in some people's thinking, it is much more probable that the South led the nation in withdrawing from the public schools primarily because the South is also the Bible belt. Many of the Christian schools, like the one at Grace Baptist, were sponsored by integrated churches.

The Supreme Court had introduced the phrase "separation of church and state" into the Everson v. Board of Education case of 1947. The phrase is not found in the Constitution, but was lifted from a letter from Thomas Jefferson to the Danbury Baptists. In the letter, Jefferson had written to ensure the Baptists that the government would not force a state church upon them. The 1947 case introduced this nuclear-powered phrase into Supreme Court case precedent, but for 14 years it lay dormant. Then in 1962 the Engel v. Vitale case removed prayer from the schools. This case further ingrained the false spin on the phrase "separation of church and state" into the court system as case precedent, and in rapid fashion numerous other religious liberties were violently stripped away. Taking the Bible and prayer out of schools created a significant demand for more Bible-based, privately run Christian schools.

Yet another factor which drove parents toward private schools was sex education in the public schools. Dennis Wiggs was pastoring First Free Will Baptist Church in Beaufort, North Carolina, in 1972. One Wednesday evening as he approached the church, an extremely irate deacon approached him on the sidewalk. The deacon's daughter had been subjected to the sex education class that day in the public school. Pastor Wiggs couldn't believe what he was hearing. He made some phone calls and received permission to sit in on the sex education class the next day. Again, he was shocked at what was being promoted as he listened to the woman make her presentation.

Pastor Wiggs wrote a letter to the Board of Education and made arrangements to attend the next BOE meeting. Somehow, word had gotten out about his letter; and when he arrived, he found the place packed. He waited through the meeting; and when it appeared that they were going to adjourn without addressing his letter, he spoke up and reminded the chairman that he had sent a letter. The letter had been conveniently misplaced, but Pastor Wiggs was prepared for such a maneuver. He calmly said, "That's ok, I have a copy of it right here." He then publicly read his letter.

The upshot of it was that the chairman dodged the public pressure by appointing Pastor Wiggs and a half dozen others to a committee charged with investigating the concerns. It quickly became obvious that the committee wasn't going to do much. During the weeks when Pastor Wiggs was attending committee meetings, people in the community were approaching him about starting a Christian school. Finally, it came to the point that he stood at a Board meeting and announced, "I appreciate you people in here. You have really helped me. You have convinced me that I need to start a Christian school." He then excused himself and left.

Wiggs was still a young preacher in 1972, just a few years out of Bible college. He knew nothing about starting Christian schools. The fact is, in those early days, very few pastors knew much about starting and operating schools. In spite of this, he talked to the deacons and found that First FWB of Beaufort was enthusiastically in favor of starting a school.

Next, he contacted a friend in Goldsboro, North Carolina. Lorenza Stox was also young, but he had been the principal at Faith Christian Academy in Goldsboro for the few years since he had gotten out of college. Goldsboro is about 100 miles west of Beaufort and was the home of one of the earliest Christian schools in the area, Goldsboro Christian School, which was started by 2nd Baptist Church of Goldsboro in 1963. A leader from that school later went over to Faith Free Will Baptist and helped start Faith Christian Academy.

Lorenza Stox was the first principal of the Academy, and he sent Wiggs copies of curriculum, such as they had at that time: schedules, guide books - everything he thought would help another church get a school started. He also came to Beaufort and spoke to the church leaders. Stox would go on to pastor churches, then to serve first as Dean, and later as President, of Southeastern FWB college. He demonstrated this interest in helping churches prepare to educate others early on when, as a young principal at Faith Christian Academy, he assisted several churches in starting Christian schools.

With Lorenza Stox's help, Beaufort FWB started their Christian school in 1972. Other churches mentioned in this book had already started schools as well. Pastor Wingard and Calvary Baptist in New Bern had begun Calvary Christian School in 1969. Grace Baptist in Morehead City started Grace Christian School in 1970. Each church had their own motivations for taking on the tremendous workload and expense of a Christian school; but the demand was great, and the churches stepped up to supply the much needed ministries.

Few churches had any experience in the world of education outside their Sunday School and Bible classes. There was no one publishing a full set of textbooks and curriculum for private Bible-based schools. Pensacola Christian College would become a leader in training educators later; but they didn't open until 1974. Bob Jones University was working to meet this need; providing some teaching material but the whole movement was in its infancy. The teaching materials were often in the form of handouts, not textbooks and professionally prepared materials. Yet, what they provided was tremendously helpful.

Some churches were blessed to have retired public school teachers who would agree to teach. Otherwise, most of the teachers were young graduates fresh out of Bible colleges, but these graduates had not been specifically trained to be educators.

Independent Baptists and Free Will Baptists worked closely together in the Christian School movement. There was a strong "agree to disagree agreeably" spirit and numerous lifelong friendships were formed. This is remarkable considering that some Independent Baptist churches were formed when Free Will Baptist members pulled out of their churches to start churches which taught eternal security. On the other hand, Faith Christian Academy of Goldsboro was started in a FWB church after a leader left an Independent Baptist Church. An example of this spirit of cooperation is found in a Christian Education magazine called The Scope which the Free Will Baptists then published on a bimonthly basis. Pastor Wiggs wrote a cover page article for the September - October 1973 edition in which he told about how Beaufort Christian School was started. That same issue also dedicates a full page to advertising and promoting a Mid-America Sunday School convention where the Independent Baptist pastor, Jack Hyles, was the first speaker listed.

So, regardless of how or why the various Christian schools got started, they did start. They overcame obstacles, the lack of experience, the lack of trained teachers, the lack of professionally prepared curriculum and they began! And God blessed it. A 1980 report from the North Carolina Division of Non-Public Education estimates that from 1968 to 1972 private school enrollment in North Carolina nearly tripled, going from approximately 18,000 to 50,000 students.

An example of how the Christian schools were a blessing in some churches is found in Calvary Baptist Church of Greenville where

95

Brother Bobby Thomas pastored for 42 years. When asked, "What is the greatest thing you've ever seen God do?" Brother Thomas spoke of the spirit of revival that swept through Calvary Baptist as they got their Christian school started. Parents were so excited to have a Godly option for their children that the enthusiasm spilled over into the church services for the next 8-10 years. Calvary Baptist in turn helped three other churches start Christian schools. Ironically, despite all the accusations that the Christian School movement was racially motivated, one of the three schools which were started with Calvary Baptist's assistance was hosted by a church where all the members were black. To the glory of God, these Christian schools *continue to this day.*

Getting something new started often comes with an exciting rush of adrenaline. The first step is *a work of faith* as believers step out. But that *work* must transition into a *labor of love* in order for it to be maintained. Keeping the Christian schools going has proved to be a major challenge. There will be more on that in a later chapter when we get to the late 70s.

But before that challenge to the Christian schools would come to a head in 1977, God would initiate two other great ministries where the Word of God would literally take to the air.

Chapter Eleven

1973 Start of Mission Aeroservices

In 1973, God would see fit to raise up yet another ministry out of Calvary Baptist Church in New Bern, but this story actually begins in Wilmington, North Carolina. A young man named Jack had begun to date a young lady named Jonnie. Jonnie had been saved a couple of years earlier in Jacksonville, Florida, but was not attending church; yet she witnessed to Jack on their first date. Jack and Jonnie were married in March of 1964. One of Jonnie's coworkers had been inviting her to go to Grace Baptist Church of Wilmington. Jack wasn't very interested, but Jonnie wanted them to go to church together. He finally agreed to go. Pastor Ray Noland preached a sermon on hell that first Sunday, and Jack thought, "Man, I won't be coming back here!"

But God was working, and Jack did go back. He was under conviction, but not moving. He worked for the telephone company and had a couple of close calls as he was traveling on the highway making service calls. After one of the near accidents, the question nagged him, "Jack, where would you be right now if that log truck had hit you head on?" On the first Sunday morning in November 1964, Jack went to church with Jonnie again. Evangelist Bill Compton was preaching; and when the invitation was given, Jack noticed tears starting to well up in Jonnie's eyes. Then she went forward. Jack was totally confused by that. He thought that people only went to the altar to be saved; he didn't realize that Christians also went forward to pray for other people, or other matters. He knew she was already saved. If anyone in the building was saved and on their way to heaven, he was confident it was she. He thought, "It's not her that needs to be down there; it's me that needs to be down there!"

Like many, Jack had a false impression that if his good deeds outweighed his bad he'd make it into heaven. He pictured it like a cigar box with his bad deeds on one side and gold stars for his good deeds on the other. That morning, the thought occurred to him: "Everything in the box is black, and Jesus is the gold star of glory. If I receive Him, I won't be worrying about this balancing; 'cause when Jesus goes on the scale, He's going to outweigh all the black ones. If I receive Him, He takes care of it."

Next thing Jack knew, he was walking the aisle. He left Grace Baptist Church of Wilmington that day as a new man in Christ Jesus, the righteousness of Christ having been imputed to his account. Jack and Jonnie Hunt grew in the Lord while Jack continued working with the telephone company. For the next nine years, he served as a Sunday School teacher, usher, deacon, and Bus Pastor. Sister Jonnie helped in the Christian school, taught Sunday School, and worked in the bus ministry. The Lord was working, and they surrendered to the Lord to do anything He wanted them to do.

Jack is an Air Force veteran, having worked electronic maintenance in a Strategic Air Command Communications Center in Morocco when America had Boeing B-47 Stratojet bombers stationed there during the Cold War nuclear alert. In 1959, during his tour of duty there, he also learned to fly through the Air Force Flying Club. When he returned to America, he taught an electronics maintenance course at Keesler Air Force Base in Mississippi.

After his military service, his love for aviation led him to earn his Commercial Pilot and Flight Instructor licenses. For a time, he worked as a part-time flight instructor at the Wilmington airport. Then, God began to coordinate meetings which would change the Hunt's lives. Jack had met some missionary pilots and had even flown to Winston-Salem to pick up missionary pilot J. T. Lyons to bring him to Wilmington. Also, at an International Fellowship of Fundamental Baptists (IFFB) meeting, Pastor Noland invited Bill Wingard from Calvary Baptist in New Bern to preach. He preached on "Rehoboam and Jeroboam, those 'Boam Boys." Brother Hunt fellowshipped with Pastor Wingard after the service and instantly liked him.

Brother Jack began to sense a real need. Missionaries requiring air transportation needed to be taught flying in rugged third-world mission environments. They needed a support network which could help get aircraft parts to them. Sometimes aircraft repairs, upgrades, and modifications required teams who could travel to perform the maintenance on-site.

After prayer about who to contact concerning starting such a ministry, Brother Jack made arrangements to meet with Lee Roberson, the pastor at Highland Park Baptist Church and the head of Tennessee Temple University. The meeting also included Dr. Tom Freeney, the General Director of Baptist International Missions Inc. (BIMI). He presented his idea of a ministry which would help train missionary pilots and would assist them in maintaining their qualifications. Both men liked his ideas and expressed interest. However, Dr. Freeney felt that it should be handled through the school since it was training related, while Dr. Roberson felt it should be handled through BIMI since it was missions related. Unfortunately, their interest in the idea fell into the gap between the two men's opinions, and nothing ever occurred at BIMI or Tennessee Temple University to get a ministry started. Brother Hunt harbored no ill will toward the two men. He knew that such a ministry would be an expensive and daunting undertaking. He was just sharing his burden.

But this didn't mean God wasn't working. He simply had other plans. Jack Hunt got word that Bill Wingard was also a licensed pilot and that Brother Wingard owned a Piper Cherokee 235 which he used in the ministry. He called Brother Wingard just to chat about airplanes. He asked if Pastor Wingard had considered using his airplane for missions. As the conversation continued, he learned that Pastor Wingard, along with Pastors Bell, Eborn, and Winstead, had just recently formed World Wide New Testament Baptist Missions. Before the conversation ended, Pastor Wingard had invited him to come and present his ideas for a ministry to the mission board.

The men on the mission board considered his request and then asked him to come back to speak at their next board meeting. After the meeting concluded, Pastor Wingard asked, "Would you pray and ask the Lord if He would have you come and develop an aviation ministry with us? We believe that the man with the burden is the man that ought to be doing it." The Hunts agreed to pray about the matter.

As we have seen repeatedly, God was once again working simultaneously on other aspects of the vision as well. While the

WWNTBM board and the Hunts, were praying about whether to start a missionary aviation ministry, an aircraft mechanic named Les Womack contacted Pastor Bill Wingard and said he was interested in working on missionary airplanes.

Jack and Jonnie had already committed themselves to do whatever God wanted them to do with their lives, and they felt like this opportunity was opening for them because this was the path He wanted them to walk. They committed to the missionary aviation ministry, were interviewed, and then accepted by WWNTBM in November of 1973, making them the third missionaries to sign on with World Wide New Testament Baptist Missions.

But after making the commitment, a normal and natural nervousness set in. They would be leaving a secure job where Jack had twelve years seniority. Also, they would be leaving their home and the security they enjoyed to go on deputation and to trust churches to send their support. Their families were against them stepping into this insecure world. Jonnie experienced chest pains. It seemed that, like the children of Israel at Kadesh-Barnea, the devil was telling her, "You'll never go. You'll never enter into Canaan."

Jack was also having his doubts. He had already submitted his two-week notice. On one of his last days on the job, he was eating a hot dog at lunch time. He needed a blessing, and the thought came to him to go to Ephesians chapter one because, as he recalled, "If you can't get your heart blessed there, there ain't no blessing to be had."

As he read, God began to use the scripture to reaffirm that what was happening in their lives was God's leading and that God would take care of them. He read and thought: Ephesians 1:4 ...*according as He hath chosen us in Him...* "That's good, God chose me for this." Ephesians 1:13 ...*sealed with the Holy Spirit of promise...* "I'm safe in Him." 1:19 ...*according to the working of His mighty power.* "He's going

101

to take care of us." But it seemed as if the devil answered, "You're just trying to make something out of that." He flipped over a couple more pages and Ephesians 4:1 seemed to jump off the page ...*walk worthy of the vocation wherewith ye are called."* He thought, "Flight instructing is a vocation!" Then God gave a final assurance with Ephesians 4:11, *And He gave some, apostles; and some, prophets; and some, evangelists; and some, pastors and* "Flight instructors!" *(teachers)!*

Excited, Jack called Jonnie to let her know that God had granted him peace about the decision they had made. Once more, our omnipresent Lord had been at work at both locations at the same time. Jonnie had also found peace through the scriptures that very same morning. In her case, God used Psalm 37, specifically verses 3-5 *Trust in the LORD, and do good; so shalt thou dwell in the land...* She thought, "Praise the Lord, I WILL enter into Canaan." *...and verily thou shalt be fed.* "He will take care of us!" *Delight thyself also in the LORD; and He shall give thee the desires of thine heart* (more on this later). *Commit thy way unto the LORD; trust also in Him, and He shall bring it to pass.* Psalm 37:23 continued; *The steps of a good man are ordered by the LORD...* On the same day, God granted each of them peace through His Word. They knew they had made the right decision.

They went on deputation, but times were tough. No one had heard much of the fledgling World Wide New Testament Baptist Missions agency yet. But opportunities to train pilots and work on airplanes began to open up quickly. God provided, in spite of the fact that throughout their fifty years of ministry, the Hunts never achieved more than 74% of the support recommended by their sending church and the mission board. Until their house sold in Wilmington, they had two house payments, one in Wilmington and one in New Bern. Fifty years later, Mrs. Jonnie's voice still cracked and her eyes welled with tears as she remembered going to the mailbox when they didn't have the money for the mortgage payments and finding a $10 check and an encouraging note from Evangelist Dolphus Price and a $250 check from Grace Baptist Church in Wilmington.

When their house in Wilmington sold, the Hunts used the equity to buy their first airplane, a little Cessna 150. They now had an airplane, other aircraft to work on, and pilots to train, but nowhere to work *from*. They found that they could rent space at the local New Bern Simmons-Nott airport.

The Simmons in the name of the airport referred to a New Bern native, Senator Furnifold Simmons, who is partially responsible for our federal income taxes. In 1909, there was a push for a tax on income over about $400,000 in today's money. Conservatives attempted to use reverse psychology and squash the idea by going along with it. In order to silence proponents of the tax, they introduced a constitutional amendment, sure that it would never be ratified. But to their chagrin, the 16th amendment WAS ratified. Afterward Representative Oscar Underwood and Senator Simmons introduced the Underwood Tariff Act. It lowered tariffs, but it also had the dubious distinction of reinstating the federal income tax which had been declared unconstitutional prior to the ratification of the 16th amendment. The airport is now known as the Coastal Carolina Regional Airport (EWN).

Since the new aviation ministry had to rent hangar space only on an as-needed basis, someone donated an old milk truck which they converted into a rolling tool box. This gift provided them with a permanent place for a work bench and to store their tools and equipment.

Jack Hunt learned that Forest Minges, the owner of the local Pepsi bottling company, had a small but very nice private airport. Hunt contacted him to enquire about renting space. At the time, Jack wasn't aware that Forest Minges was one of the people who had gotten saved in the '58 revival. Minges told him, "You can keep your airplane there for $15 per month. You can rent hangar space for $90 per month. Mr. Minges had also installed a mobile home for another flight instructor to use, but that instructor only stayed for two months. Forest Minges offered to rent that trailer to them for an additional $100 per month.

Jack Hunt started to interrupt. There was no way they could afford those prices at that time, but Mr. Minges continued: "Now, if anybody asks, that's what you're paying to be out here... just like anybody else. However, what I donate to your ministry is nobody's business, and I'm going to give it back to you." And so, the Hunt's moved what was then called The Academy of Missionary Aviation (AMA) to the Minges's property, which was known as the "Pepsi International Airport." Each month they wrote out a rent check for $205. In turn, each month Mr. Minges wrote out a check making a $205 donation to their ministry.

This arrangement continued and worked very well for about four years, but then Mr. Minges passed away suddenly from a heart attack. As his sons worked to maintain the family business, they stopped returning the monthly payments which the aviation ministry was making. The mission funds quickly dropped down to the point that Jack had to contact the heirs and work out a plan where they could keep the plane there and rent hangar space on an as-needed basis, but they had to let the rented office and classroom go. The AMA office found its way into the Hunt's small home. One file cabinet had to be relocated into Mrs. Jonnie's tiny kitchen. The

Minges brothers told the Hunts that they would try to start giving them some of the money back after they made it to the end of the year and confirmed that the business finances were stable.

As they struggled and began investigating other options, Mrs. Jonnie started praying that God would give them the airport. Brother Jack rebuked her: "That's covetousness. You can't ask God to give us something that belongs to somebody else. You can ask for one like it, but you're going to get in trouble." Mrs. Jonnie didn't share his conviction. She retorted, "You pray like you want to, and I'll pray like I want to."

Then one day, as Jack was gassing up their car, he saw a large sign saying there was 400-plus acres for sale. His heart sank. It was the Minges property and it included the airport. Now, they definitely would have to find a new location for the ministry. But then, as if God spoke to him, a thought came out of the blue. "If they have it up for sale, it's no longer covetousness to pray for it. They want to get rid of it." He called Jonnie to let her know he was going to join her in her prayers that God would somehow work out a way to purchase the airport. When she asked what had changed his mind, Jack mischievously replied, "I saw a sign."

However, when he contacted the Minges family to see what the price would be just for the airport, they told him they couldn't break up the property. The airport was right in the middle, and the right of way to it would mar the rest of the property, making it more difficult to sell.

As with Ernie Mills hearing Pastor Bobby Thomas preach Psalm 145:3 *Great is the Lord, and greatly to be praised,* God once again used a sermon from the psalms to encourage Jack and Jonnie Hunt. They heard Harold Sightler preach a sermon entitled, "Can God?" from Psalm 78:19." "*Can God furnish a table in the wilderness?*" The

105

congregation shouted loudly as Sightler excitedly and repeatedly proclaimed, "God can! God can!" The phrase "God can!" became a mantra for the Hunts. Brother Hunt would ask, "*Can God furnish a table in the wilderness?*" and Sister Jonnie would respond, "God Can, Yes, God Can!" As their faith grew, they added, "*Will* God furnish a table in the wilderness?" and the other would respond, "Yes, God Can, and God Will!" This went on for quite some time. Incredibly, although they literally couldn't afford to pay rent on even a portion of the airport, they began to have a peace that God was actually going to make a way for the airport to belong to the ministry.

Then, one day Jack came in for lunch and Jonnie told him Pastor Wingard wanted him to call right away. Jack was surprised because he knew that Pastor Wingard was in a WWNTBM board meeting. Huge waves had recently devasted much of the island of Majuro in the Marshall Islands, and the board was having an emergency meeting as they were trying to figure out how to help the missionaries.

Jack called and Pastor Wingard asked him to come to the board meeting right away. His first reaction was, "What have I done, or what have they heard about me?" But then, God seemed to give some peace, and by the time he arrived he had convinced himself that they were going to ask him to make the trip to the island of Majuro. He had two airplane repairs in process and did not feel he could afford to take the time to go anywhere, but he silently submitted it all to the Lord's hand and walked in prepared to agree to fly to Majuro if that was how the Lord led.

When Jack walked in the door, a couple of the preachers were crying. Again, the "What do they think I have done?" thought flashed through his mind. As it turns out, the tears were tears of joy. Pastor Wingard had received a call from Mike Minges, informing him that the family had decided to **donate** the airport to the ministry! The only expense was $10 to register the deed, and the Minges family also donated the $10.

When Brother Jack came home and relayed the great news to Mrs. Jonnie and others who happened to be there at the time, it was shouting time in the Hunt household! They added a new phrase to their mantra; "God can, God will, and **God did!!**"

This all happened early in December, 1979. For tax purposes, the transaction had to be completed by the end of the year. This sent everyone scrambling to get all the requirements fulfilled in time. New Year's Eve came and found brother Vernon Henderson, "their business guy," nervously waiting in the Minges' office for the final signatures. Finally, at quarter till five the last person arrived and signed the papers. Brother Henderson sped across town to the court house to get the deed registered. There were thirteen stop lights between him and the court house, and he miraculously hit all thirteen while they were green. He arrived at five till five and found the clerk at the doors with the keys in her hand ready to lock up and presumably to begin her New Year's Eve celebrations. When Brother Henderson dashed up and insisted that he HAD to get this deed registered today, she explained that she had already put the books away. However, once more, God graciously gave favor with the right people at the right time. When she learned that the transaction had to be completed that day in order for the ministry to receive the airport, the clerk revealed that she was a Christian. She said that she would happily stay till midnight, if necessary, in order to complete *that* transaction!

God continued to bless wonderfully. Not only did the Minges family donate the 35 acres which included the 1,845 foot paved runway, the donation also included the hangar, three Quonset huts which could be used as hangars, the mobile home which had been used as an office and classroom, and the equipment necessary for maintaining the property. This equipment included both a bulldozer and a tractor with implements. There was also a fuel storage tank which the ministry had tried to buy from the Minges family; but at the time, they didn't want to sell it. Now, they gave it to them. They renamed the field Canaan Air Base, and God's assurances to Mrs. Jonnie that by faith she *would* enter into Canaan literally came true.

The ministry changed their name from Academy of Missionary Aviation to Mission Aeroservices since it became apparent that airplane maintenance was going to consume as much or more of their time than flight instructing. The constant flow of missionary pilots coming and going created a need for a house in which to host them. Jack and Jonnie Hunt had always graciously opened the doors of their own home to these missionaries, but the cramped quarters were far less than ideal. Now that the ministry owned the airport (technically it was deeded to World Wide New Testament Baptist Missions), they could explore the possibilities of adding a house to the property for the missionaries to stay.

Brother Jack mentioned the need in a prayer letter, and God once again answered prayers in an *exceeding abundantly above all that we ask or think* fashion. Help came flooding in. Pastor Mike Alvis from Heritage Baptist Church in Smithfield, Ohio, met with the men of his church. They had built their own parsonage and church building and were looking for a mission project. They decided to offer to build something instead of helping with the purchase of a trailer. They also elected to sacrifice the $25,000 they had in their parking lot fund and promised to send a team of eighteen men down to dry in the building. When they came, they brought high quality doors and windows with them as well.

The Hunt's sending church, Grace Baptist in Wilmington, donated an additional $5,000 and brought a team to pour the footers, do the brick work, and install the floor joists to have everything ready for the Heritage Baptist team. Local Christian contractors and businesses donated supplies. The father of one of World Wide's missionaries was in charge of heat and air at BJU. He came down and installed the duct work. The Hunt's son-in-law worked for a sheetrock company which donated all the interior sheetrock. An electrical code instructor from Raleigh told a contractor about the project and the contractor supplied all the electrical materials. Brother Steve Kennedy, an electrician and member of Calvary Baptist Church, wired the house with Brother Hunt's assistance. A team from a supporting church in Delaware came down and painted. A family business from Boone, North Carolina, built an 8 x 16 foot deck. A family from Maryland provided shrubbery and planted it. And Brother Hunt did everything from hanging cabinets to cutting in electrical outlets to acting as the subcontractor on the whole project. All this was done without any further requests for money or assistance beyond the original single mention of the need in the prayer letter.

But you can't outgive the Lord. A week after Pastor Alvis called and informed Brother Hunt that Heritage Baptist would give their $25,000 parking lot fund toward the missionary house, a stranger walked in to Heritage Baptist Church and donated a lot in a nearby subdivision to the church. The man had sold the lots on either side of the donated one for $30,000 each, but he donated the middle lot to the church. The church sold the donated lot within a week and once again had the money to pave its parking lot!

God has continued to bless Mission Aeroservices. Over the years, Brother Hunt and his team have performed maintenance on over eighty aircraft. Repairs have ranged from routine inspections and oil changes to major overhauls. Brother Hunt has instructed over 60 missionaries, sometimes helping them to earn their initial pilot qualifications, to upgrade their license to include instrument qualifications, or to renew their license. To those familiar with missionary aviation, a walk through Brother Hunt's photo album will reveal some recognizable names like Alaska's "Far North Flying Chaplain," and author of <u>Journey to the Edge of the Sky,</u> Les Paul Zerbe; and Bob Green.

Jack Hunt's personal experiences deserve another book. Thanks to his assistance in aerial photography and history, he was given a V.I.P. tour of MCAS Cherry Point and treated to a flight in a F-4 trainer jet with a Marine Fight Instructor. At one point they dashed to speeds nearing Mach 2 while well offshore. He has dropped Russian paratroopers in a Fairbanks, Alaska, air show. For five summers, he teamed up with Les Zerbe, flying Eskimo children to an Alaskan Bible camp on Kako Lake, off the Yukon River. At times they found themselves flying 500 miles from the nearest road. Jack has also served as an instructor in thirteen annual *Wings as Eagles* flight camps in Oshkosh, Wisconsin. These camps introduced young men to aviation and flying and encouraged them to explore the possibilities of getting involved in missionary aviation. He has also flown relief supplies into Haitian disaster areas after a hurricane and an earthquake.

Yet, in spite of such an exciting life associated with aviation, when I asked Brother Hunt, "What was the greatest thing you've ever seen God do?" he spoke of none of that. Instead, he began to tell me of an opportunity he had to preach at an Army reserve center one Sunday morning. Seven soldiers walked the aisle, some in tears, and got saved. In like fashion, Mrs. Jonnie responded to the same question in an equally humble fashion, not pointing to what they had accomplished, or the financial miracles God had performed, but rather what God was doing through some of the missionaries they had assisted. One missionary is translating the Bible in Honduras, another is having great success in Africa, establishing twelve churches in Togo. She mentioned one little Asian girl who was saved when the Hunts were sharing their ministry in a supporting church in Maryland. It is obvious that free airports and free houses haven't caused Jack and Jonnie Hunt to lose sight of the value of a single eternal soul getting saved.

Times and circumstances have changed, and decisions will have to be made regarding the future of Mission Aeroservices. Today, there are other ministries providing similar support to missionaries, whereas in 1974 they were not aware of any such ministry dedicated to assisting fundamental Bible-believing ministries. But regardless of what the future holds for Mission Aeroservices, there is no doubt that the revival that started in the 50's "***remains until this day***" through the missionaries and ministries that have been supported. As Mrs. Jonnie worded it, "It's not like you're a missionary to one place. You're a missionary to the whole world. I say we're missionaries *to the uttermost parts* (Acts 1:8)."

Although scripture refers to Satan as the *prince of the power of the air* (Ephesians 2:2), God still uses the air for His own purposes whenever He chooses. Not only did He choose to use the air to transport His missionaries, He also chose to use the air to carry radio frequencies which were dedicated to His Word.

Chapter Twelve
1975 Start of WOTJ

Around 1975, God again used a magazine article to help influence the start of a ministry. After having been saved at DuPont and then starting Grace Baptist Church, one day Pastor Clyde Eborn was reading a copy of a secular radio magazine which had been given to him by missionary Dave Arthurs, the brother who would later help Calvary Baptist of Pohnpei to start a radio station. Eborn began to be burdened for a radio station that could be used to share the gospel of Christ. Arthurs moved on to other endeavors; but Eborn traveled to Chattanooga, and a brother there helped him find an available commercial frequency. Grace Baptist Church filed the necessary paperwork to try to obtain that frequency and thus began the process of getting started in radio work.

There was endless red tape. Pastor Eborn had to spend a whole week in a Washington D.C. Federal Communications Commission (FCC) office attempting to prove that he could pastor, marry and bury people, run a church, and still run a radio station all at one time. FCC requirements dictated that they have all the radio equipment paid for and have enough money in escrow to run a station for a full year before they could be entrusted with an assigned frequency. They met with an attorney, drew up promissory notes, and by faith borrowed about $100,000. They got their approval from the FCC, but that didn't mean the battle was over.

Grace Baptist had done all the ground work to meet the FCC requirements and have the area analyzed for the frequency. They had invested tens of thousands of dollars in the process, but then a group from Kinston, North Carolina, approached and wanted to buy the frequency from them. Of course, Pastor Eborn declined, but the group wasn't through. After a period of legal maneuvering, the church's attorney called and advised Grace Baptist to get out of the fight. The other group had too much money. The attorney advised that he could get most of the money back that the church had invested if they got out in a timely fashion. Having little choice, they ceded the commercial frequency to the other group and started over.

They didn't give up. God's people don't easily walk away from a God-given burden. Dave Arthurs came back into the picture, and they learned of an opportunity to file for a frequency as an educational station. Failure is often only an opportunity to begin again more intelligently, so they filed for 90.7 F.M. This time they were both approved *and* granted the frequency assignment in a relatively short period of time. Altogether, it had taken thirteen years of praying, raising money, struggling to meet FCC requirements, and overcoming obstacles; but once they filed for the educational frequency, things moved fairly quickly. After thirteen years, they were finally getting near to putting a radio station on the air.

They began to construct a tower and studio on their church campus in Morehead City. Brother Percy Braswell, a local pastor, owned and operated a television repair shop. He put in many hours assisting with the new station, and his electronics knowledge proved to be extremely valuable. The church also had several others who had a lot of experience in different areas. In Pastor Eborn's words: "What we didn't know, we'd pray about, and just branch out and *do something*." They were also learning from the monthly issues of the *Radio World* magazine. To this day, a copy of the current edition of *Radio World* magazine can often be seen on the station manager's desk.

Since Eastern North Carolina is a hurricane prone area, engineers recommended that they construct a solid steel tower. Volunteers dug the footings and poured the concrete; then a tower company erected the 400' structure. Things appeared to be going well, but nothing is ever easy when the prince of the power of the air doesn't want his airwaves used for the broadcasting of the gospel. The construction crew did not have the 6" hangers that the plans called for to attach the transmission line, so they substituted longer hangers. Apparently, these longer hangers sagged under the weight of the 400' transmission line. After a period of time, this flaw caused the line to separate at one of the connections near the top rendering the entire outfit inoperable. Repairs had to be made. But at the time of construction, all seemed to be moving forward in a timely manner.

Pastor Eborn, his nephew Dwayne, and another man rode to Georgia to purchase a radio transmitter. On the way back, they stopped by Bob Jones University and toured the studios there. Incredibly, after thirteen years of effort, this visit to Bob Jones was actually the first time Clyde Eborn had ever stepped foot inside a radio studio. The experts in the radio work there advised Eborn that he'd never make it with volunteer help. With all due respect for the great work that has been done at Bob Jones University over the years, this advice calls to mind a quote from Henry Ford. Ford said: "If ever I wanted to kill opposition by unfair means, I would endow the opposition with experts." BJU was not in opposition to the new station by any means. They were quite helpful, but Ford's quote illustrates that sometimes advice from experts can be discouraging. Thankfully, Pastor Eborn and Grace Baptist Church continued despite the "expert counsel," and God did indeed help them to function well with a staff comprised primarily of volunteers.

Another significant event happened on that Georgia trip. Pastor Eborn asked his nephew Dwayne to consider coming on staff as full-time station manager. Dwayne, the son of Clyde Eborn's brother Jim, had grown up in Grace Baptist Church (note: At birth Eborn was misspelled on Jim's birth certificate, so he and his family spell their last name Ebron instead of Eborn). As a teenager, Dwayne kept hearing all the excitement about getting a radio station on the air, and had bought an FM radio specifically for the purpose of being able to hear it when it happened. That radio sat unused for years, but now the time was close. After prayer, Dwayne resigned from a well-paying job at Piedmont Airlines and accepted the position of Station Manager for the new radio work.

Finally, on the afternoon of Monday, December 12, 1988, WOTJ went live at the 90.7 F.M. frequency! Brother Percy Braswell and others were working on the equipment. Pastor Eborn and his wife had gone on board the base at Cherry Point to make a visit. Someone called and let them know that WOTJ was on the air. Pastor Eborn sat in the home where he was visiting and wept. Thirteen years of prayer, frustration, and labor had finally come to fruition. The assigned call letters of WOTJ were declared to stand for: "**W**inning **O**thers **T**o **J**esus." This is an apt description of their purpose.

Those first years of radio work were labor intensive. Computers were just starting to become affordable in 1988. Microsoft Windows had just been released in 1985, and personal computers as we now know them were new to planet earth. At that time, only about 10% of American households owned a personal computer. The radio station owned none, so everything had to be done manually. Programs and music were on reel-to-reel tapes. Brother Dwayne worked from 6:00 a.m. until WOTJ signed off at 11:00 p.m., managing four reel-to-reel machines. It was necessary to find the start of each song or program, then roll the tape back just enough so that when he queued it up, the tape started at the beginning of the song or sermon. All programming was live. There was no opportunity to edit mistakes.

Then the tower was struck by lightning. Pastor Eborn was just pulling in the church parking lot about sunset and physically saw it happen. There was a terrible storm in process, and suddenly the tower "lit up like a Christmas tree for just a second." Although the tower was well grounded with copper rods which were each several feet long and were driven deep into the ground at every guy-wire as well as in multiple other places, the complex grounding system wasn't adequate to absorb the impressive power of the lightning strike. The lightning ran through the electrical lines and into the studio. Decades later, Pastor Eborn chuckled at the memory of seeing the studio door burst open and Brother Dwayne and others sprinting frantically out into the storm. Pastor Eborn saw it, but Dwayne heard it. "There was a lot of popping and frying and sizzling inside those components. We could hear stuff just frying and popping inside!" Once again, the members of the church were forced to scramble and make repairs, but WOTJ was soon back on the air, Winning Others To Jesus.

But lightning strikes weren't the only opposition the thriving churches who were experiencing *revival that remained* faced back then. In Raleigh, there was growing momentum toward forcing the fledgling Christian schools to conform to government mandates.

Chapter Thirteen

Fight for the Christian Schools - 1977

In 2016, several Independent Baptist pastors visited the Legislative building in Raleigh. They were with a group called Awake America which encourages pastors to simply visit with their state legislators and to pray with them. A couple dozen pastors were present that day because North Carolina was embroiled in the "bathroom bill" debate: Would transgenders be allowed to use the bathroom of their choice or would they be required to use the bathroom which corresponded to their gender at birth? Pastor Tim Butler, pastor of People's Baptist Church in Greenville, North Carolina had taken the initiative in encouraging other Independent Baptist pastors to participate. Pastor Bill Wingard, 82 years old at the time, was one of the pastors who had answered the call and made the 2 ½ hour trip to Raleigh.

Brother Butler noticed that Pastor Wingard had a very troubled look on his face. Concerned for his well-being, Pastor Butler discreetly worked his way alongside Pastor Wingard and quietly asked, "Are you OK?" Wingard responded, "The last time I was up here I was on trial. They told me you need to be prepared to leave here and go to jail." What follows in this chapter is the story that led to one of North Carolina's finest and most law-abiding citizens being threatened with jail.

The fight for the existence of Christian schools that erupted in 1977 really began with the Brown v. Topeka Board of Education case decisions in 1954-1955. The original decision declared segregation unconstitutional; then a 1955 follow-on court ruling ordered public schools to desegregate "with all deliberate speed." This decision led to forced busing, and many southern politicians vowed to find ways to circumvent the law imposed by the Supreme Court. In Virginia, Senator Harry Byrd organized a plan known as "Massive Resistance." North Carolina's spin on this idea was "The Pearsall Plan." In a nutshell, the Pearsall Plan involved rewriting state laws so that private schools would come under the oversight of the Department of Public Education and would have to meet all the same requirements as public schools. All public schools would then be made into private schools, and parents would be given vouchers to send their children to these "private schools." The "benefit" of this would be that the private schools being held in the same buildings, with the same teachers, and still funded by taxpayer dollars, would not have to comply with the desegregation mandates placed on the public schools.

The Pearsall plan was enacted and the laws were changed; but quite predictably, these laws were promptly challenged in court and declared to be unconstitutional. The resistance to forced integration failed; however, the laws requiring private schools to meet all the requirements of public schools were never revoked. Like the introduction of the church-and-state clause, these dangerous new requirements that private schools had to meet all the same requirements as public schools lay dormant for several years. The new laws were not enforced.

But then, a seed was planted and slowly began to grow. In 1961, North Carolina created a new office called The Division of Non-Public Education. In 1963 they began publishing lists of approved and non-approved private schools, but they did nothing to penalize the unapproved schools for noncompliance. By the early 70's, the annual report that private schools had to complete had grown to 13 pages long. These long reports reflected "a feeling of growing mistrust and dislike for private education among officials in the Department of Public Education," as David Morgan would word it in his 1980 Division of Non-Public Education report entitled <u>History of Private School Regulation in North Carolina</u>. The intensity of this feeling is reflected in a statement that Morgan also recorded which was made by the Department of Education's publicity director, Tom Davis. Davis "deplored the State's inability to regulate the schools effectively... because *it's not fair to the State to say that a child that goes through these gosh-awful schools is a citizen.*"

The fledgling Christian schools slowly became more aware that they were technically required to meet all the same requirements as the public schools, and that they were not in compliance with the law. They also began to become very concerned because of the growing push for them to be forced to comply.

There were several areas where the Christian school leaders had every reason to be concerned if the state ever chose to aggressively enforce the laws. One issue was teacher certification. This requirement would prevent Christian schools from hiring teachers straight from out-of-state Bible colleges. Most of these Bible colleges were not accredited in a way that the state of North Carolina would recognize.

There were also compulsory attendance rules. Technically, any student attending an unapproved private school was in violation of these compulsory attendance laws. There were additional concerns regarding the mandatory testing requirements. If private school students were required to take the same tests and answer the same questions as the public school students before they could graduate, it would force the private schools to teach the same godless curriculum which had motivated them to start the private schools to begin with. The list went on, and pastors and Christian school leaders became more and more concerned about the state oversight of the private schools.

In 1974, the North Carolina General Assembly appointed Senator Tom Strickland to chair a study of the private school concerns, with a focus on the teacher certification issue. The Strickland Commission became a lightning rod for the Christian school movement, and for the first time private schools mobilized in opposition to the state's regulation. Reverend Kent Kelly, a pastor and school administrator from Southern Pines, North Carolina, traveled over 5,000 miles visiting every Christian school in North Carolina in 2 ½ weeks, earning him the nickname of "the Paul Revere of the Christian school revolution." The result was that he appeared before the Strickland Commission with 10,000 signatures "seeking relief from any connection with public education and the Office of the Superintendent of Public Instruction." When all was said and done, the State pretty well maintained status quo in spite of the recommendations of the Strickland Commission.

Then in 1977, things came to a head. Fundamentalist school leaders consulted with constitutional attorney William Ball, who had recently won a case before the Supreme Court involving an Amish community in Wisconsin who were removing their children from public schools at age 14. After meeting with Mr. Ball, 83 fundamentalist schools represented by three Christian school organizations, chose not to submit their required reports for the year. In addition to the Amish case, they were also emboldened by an Ohio case in which the Supreme Court had ruled in favor of Christian schools. In April 1977, the state filed suit in Wake County against eleven schools which represented the 83 schools that declined to comply with the reporting requirements.

While the regulation lawsuit began to unfold, the state also pushed aggressively for Standardized Testing in both public and private schools. This was an additional sticking point as Christian school leaders found some of the questions to be "morally offensive." A public meeting was conducted, and over 500 North Carolina citizens showed up. There were 66 speakers, only two of which were in favor of the Standardized Testing in private schools. No State Board of Education members bothered to attend the meeting, and in their next meeting the BOE voted to impose the standardized tests on private schools.

The private school organizations filed suit, and on April 26, 1978, between 4,000 and 5,000 supporters showed up outside the Wake County Courthouse. In spite of the public support for the Christian schools, the Wake County court ruled in favor of the State.

The schools then appealed to the North Carolina State Supreme Court, but before the case could be reheard, the General Assembly intervened. After a tremendous lobbying effort, the 1979 General

Assembly revoked the 1955 Pearsall Plan law which required private schools to comply with the same regulations as public schools. They replaced the Pearsall Plan law with two laws, one for private schools and one for public schools. The new requirements were acceptable to the Christian school leaders. In addition, Governor James Hunt moved the Department of Non-Public Education out from under the State Board of Education and placed it under the Office of the Governor. Thankfully, these legislative actions meant that Bill Wingard as well as other pastors and Christian school administrators never went to jail in North Carolina.

There have been few lengthy quotes in this book, preference being given to telling the stories of the individuals involved instead. However, the summary written by David Morgan in his 1980 History of Private School Regulation in North Carolina report bears repeating. Morgan wrote:

> The history of private school regulation in North Carolina, in many ways, is the story of bureaucracy at its worst. It shows how needless regulations become accepted; how they are made needlessly more complex and burdensome; and how the very fact of their existence comes to be taken as proof of their usefulness. It shows how officials of administrative agencies - even, in certain cases, officials who are popularly elected - tend to become remote and grow insensitive to expressions of public interest and concern; and how they sometimes consider it their duty to work against segments of the public they should be trying to serve. On the other hand, the history of the regulation controversy, especially in its most recent chapters, can be seen as a vindication of those closest to the avenues of real political power - in the General Assembly and

123

in the Governor's office - and of their role as by-passers around the bottlenecks of bureaucratic intolerance and insensitivity: for those persons, whether willingly or reluctantly, eventually conformed to the will of the private citizens most vitally affected by this issue.

It was surprisingly difficult to find pastors and Christian school leaders who could provide their personal experiences in this fight for the Christian schools. Most remembered it, but downplayed their own role. Pastor Dennis Wiggs summarized this attitude with the comment: "We knew it was a battle, but I didn't see anybody getting too upset. They just trusted God."

Was it all worthwhile? In the 1770s, a spirit of revival was a factor in American patriots choosing to fight in the Revolutionary War shortly after the Great Awakening. Two hundred years later, a spirit of revival burned in Eastern North Carolina in the 50s and 60s and was a factor in Christians rallying for the cause of freedom once again in the 1970s. Do the *effects of that revival remain unto this day?* Here are just three somewhat random examples of the quality of the servants of the Lord that Eastern North Carolina Christian schools have helped produce since the "Christian School Revolution" of 1977.

Pastor Brian Ernsberger was saved though the bus ministry of Calvary Baptist Church in New Bern, and then graduated from Calvary Baptist Church School in 1979. Over the past 24 years he has pastored three churches in the state of Washington and in Montana. Pastor Brian Alphin also graduated from Calvary Baptist Church School of New Bern in 2004 and then graduated Pensacola Christian College in 2008. He has planted Lighthouse Baptist Church in Washington, North Carolina (which locals proudly refer to as "the original Washington"). Another example is April Wood, who attended Christian schools in Eastern North Carolina while her father was stationed at MCAS Cherry Point. She went on to graduate from Sheets Memorial Christian School in Lexington, North Carolina as the salutatorian. She then graduated from Pensacola Christian College *summa cum laude.* She has served as a North Carolina judge and ran for a seat on the state Supreme Court in 2022. The list goes on. We thank God for the foundations that Christian schools have provided for these and many other young folks!

Unfortunately, the Christian school movement continues to be one of the most beleaguered ministries of the local churches. Pastor Dennis Wiggs started the Beaufort Christian Academy and then later pastored Ruth's Chapel Free Will Baptist Church in New Bern. Ruth's Chapel had an existing Christian school which thrived under his leadership. In spite of these successes, each of these schools were promptly shut down by pastors who followed Brother Wiggs. Grace Christian School of Morehead City (then later of Newport), did well under Pastor Eborn's leadership; but amid declining enrollment due to Covid, he led the church to shut the school down after a full fifty years. The church endorsed home schooling instead.

Thankfully some of the other schools are still thriving, but there is a danger that this generation of American Christians will let some of the religious freedoms that our forefathers fought for slip away through neglect. The freedom to have a Bible-based education may die if our generation does not fully appreciate how the previous generation fought for it. "***To some extent, that revival continues until this day***" in the Christian schools: but will the next generation be able to say that?

But thankfully, while some ministries were struggling for survival, others were thriving and growing.

Chapter Fourteen

1993 - The Fundamental Broadcasting Network Started

God continued to bless at Grace Baptist Church in Morehead City and the radio station it had hosted since 1988. Between 1988 and 1993, technology and equipment improved, Grace Baptist Church continued to grow, and more and more volunteers became involved in the radio work.

Pastor Eborn found himself repeatedly praying that God would make WOTJ a "mother station," even though he really didn't know exactly what that would entail. Pastors from other churches would come to the coast on vacation and tour the station. Repeatedly, they would comment that they would like for their church to host a station; but when they saw the amount of work involved, they knew they could never get enough volunteer help to host a full station themselves. WOTJ had 20-25 volunteers pulling shifts and preparing the programming. The pastors began to inquire about the possibilities of WOTJ feeding their programming to them; that way they wouldn't have to duplicate all the work of putting the programming together. Some suggested they would like to use some of WOTJs programming, but to also have the flexibility of substituting some of their own local programming as well.

In response to these requests, the staff at WOTJ began to explore options. They learned of satellite feeds, but they were outrageously expensive. Then, a new technology using frequency delivery became available. This new technology allowed signals to be sent to, and received from, satellites much more economically. Again, Pastor Eborn led Grace Baptist Church and WOTJ to a great step of faith. They borrowed money to install equipment to feed WOTJ'S programming to a satellite. And once again, God was ahead of them, simultaneously working on both ends of the problem at the same time. While Pastor Eborn was praying that God would make WOTJ a "mother station" and taking steps of faith to make it possible, a young couple and a pastor in West Virginia were each burdened separately to have Christian radio in their area.

Mike Tyler and his wife Kelly were praying fervently for Christian radio in the Summersville, West Virginia area. Mike taught electronics and also owned and operated a small business called Two Way Radio. He and his wife refinanced their home and purchased property on a summit called Beech Knob where a tower could be constructed. Beech Knob is approximately 20 miles southeast of Summersville and at an elevation of 4,137 feet; it is one of the highest summits in the area.

God was also working in the heart of a local pastor, giving him a burden to see Christian radio come to the Summersville area. That pastor was Jim Fellure who was pastoring Mountain State Baptist

Church in Summersville at that time. God led Mike and Kelly Tyler to Mountain State Baptist and things began to move forward. Construction began on a tower on Beech Knob, a transmitter was purchased, and an application was submitted for a license.

In 1993, their license was approved by the FCC, but during the time that had elapsed as they awaited approval; Pastor Fellure had resigned. A new pastor came to Mountain State Baptist. The new pastor had been involved in radio work with the Roloff ministries in Texas, and he quickly recognized that Mountain State did not have the money, facilities, nor personnel to operate their own radio station. He had already had some previous communications with station manager Dwayne Ebron at WOTJ in Morehead City, North Carolina, so he reached out to Dwayne now to discuss what to do with the Summersville station.

The folks at WOTJ received the call to help Mountain State Baptist Church in Summersville. God knew Mountain State had a license for a radio station. God also knew that WOTJ had a signal going to a satellite and that signal needed a receptor. At this point all He had to do was to get the two together. After meeting with the folks from WOTJ, Mountain State Baptist Church elected to *give* their license to WOTJ! It had taken thirteen years of love, sweat, prayers, and financial sacrifice to get 90.7 FM on the air, now a second frequency was *given* to them in a matter of weeks!

Mountain State also donated a portion of their church campus so that a studio could be installed for the radio station. The signal would be received there, mixed with local programming, and then sent by microwave transmission to the tower at Beech Knob. God had been planning for this since the beginning of time. Either in creation, or in the upheaval of the earth's crust in the flood of Noah's day, the mountains of West Virginia had been conveniently arranged so that there is a clear line of transmission from the Mountain State Baptist Church campus to the tower on Beech Knob twenty miles away.

But all of this created another crisis. Grace Baptist Church and WOTJ didn't have the money for all the equipment needed to put the new affiliate on the air any more than Mountain State Baptist did. Grace Baptist and WOTJ were heavily in debt from the recent purchase of the satellite equipment. But, in yet one more step of faith, they borrowed even more money to buy the equipment needed to transmit the signal from the studio at Mountain State Baptist to Beech Knob and then in turn to transmit it out over West Virginia.

As things began to come together, Mountain State Baptist hosted a meeting of local West Virginia pastors to inform them of the new station and to solicit their support. One of the pastors was Joe Brown, who was pastoring an Independent Baptist Church in a nearby town. Brother Brown was a Vietnam veteran who had been a diver with a Navy Underwater Demolition Team (the predecessors to the Navy Seals). In 1979 after his tour of duty, he had taken the electronics class that Mike Tyler had taught. But the Lord led him into the ministry instead of pursuing a career in electronics. Brother Joe had roots at Mountain State Baptist; it was the church where he had been ordained. As he sat in the meeting regarding the radio station, he liked what he heard. When the meeting concluded and they were leaving, Pastor Brown made a casual statement that would change his life. He told Brother Dwayne, "If there's anything I can do, let me know."

After prayer, Brother Dwayne and Pastor Eborn asked Brother Joe Brown to be the station manager for the West Virginia station. Mike Tyler continued serving as the station engineer, taking care of the technical side of business. Brother Joe traveled to North Carolina and learned how to run the programming. By 1993, there was still no computer automation, but technology had graduated to using a combination of compact discs and reel-to-reel tapes. Brother Brown says that when he first sat down behind the microphone in the new studio, "That mic looked like a .357 pointed at me!" It scared him to death.

On June 28, 1993, eighteen years almost to the day from when Joe Brown got saved in 1975, WMLJ went on the air in Summerville, West Virginia. They chose to declare that the call letters stood for: "**W**here **M**ountaineers **L**ove **J**esus." Indeed, the West Virginia listeners have generously and repeatedly proven the sincerity of their love over the decades that have followed.

During that first day of broadcasting, Joe Brown received a call from Pastor Eborn telling him to begin to identify as "The Fundamental Broadcasting Network" and FBN was officially born. The name was another word of faith. The "Network" consisted of exactly two stations on June 28, 1993, but God would grow it quickly.

As Pastor Eborn and Brother Dwayne were driving back from their trip to West Virginia, another phone call was made. A West Virginia man named Fred Burdette and his son had been tragically drowned in Mississippi that past spring when their boat motor failed. Winds had picked up and the boat capsized. The widowed mother, Mrs. Betty Burdette, had approached her pastor asking how she could invest some of the life insurance money in the Lord's work. Her pastor told her of the radio station in Morehead City which was trying to expand into West Virginia. Mrs. Burdette donated $50,000 to the radio station, and by the grace of God and the tender heart of a grieving mother and wife, the entire cost of the

West Virginia startup was paid for before the crew from Morehead City had even made it back to Eastern North Carolina!

WOTJ was on its way to being the "mother station" of the Fundamental Broadcasting Network. Soon after, God also opened doors for the satellite feed to go to Valley Baptist Church pastored by Brother Jim Bailey in Edinburg, Virginia; and WOTC 88.3 FM went on the air.

Not long after WOTC in Edinburg came on the air, FBN was able to install translators in both Princeton and Wilmington, North Carolina. A translator is basically a repeater which rebroadcasts FBN's signal to a new area. The translator stations require no studio or personnel, only minimal equipment needed to repeat the signal. Other affiliates also began to come on board. The affiliate stations each have their own studio, and have the option of mixing in local programming with the FBN signal before transmitting. Little by little, God has answered the prayer that WOTJ would become a "mother station." FBN has grown to two dozen affiliates in fifteen states and also has over a dozen translators in six states.

In addition to the domestic outreach, God began to open doors for international outreach as well. The first international efforts came through shortwave radio. Brother Dave Robinson, who had begun working with WOTJ while still on active duty in the Marines, had shortwave radio experience in his background as part of his military training. While in Morehead City, the Grace Baptist Church/WOTJ campus was too small to accommodate both WOTJ's tower and a shortwave transmitter. A new highway would later force them to move to a much larger campus in Newport, but government officials were still sure that the WOTJ and shortwave signals could not be broadcast from the same property without interfering with each other. Pastor Eborn convinced the government to let them try. In yet one more step of faith, they invested in and installed the shortwave equipment.

When they were ready to turn it on, the church and radio station campus was ringed with government officials and their signal monitoring equipment. The officials were shocked when they found that the signals did not interfere with each other. FBN was given the green light to begin broadcasting their programming by shortwave. Later, they would add a second shortwave frequency.

Opportunities also began to open in third world countries. A Haitian pastor visited the U.S. and heard the radio station. He got excited about it and began to enquire how he could get FBN in Haiti. With assistance from the staff at FBN, he obtained a license for a frequency in Haiti. FBN provided programming. The work in Haiti has experienced much opposition. The pastor's brother was kidnapped and killed. On a separate occasion, his son was also kidnapped but managed to escape.

The technical aspects of radio have also been challenging in Haiti. The station had been operated from a combination of generators and solar panels for years. Just recently it was converted fully to solar power. It has been difficult to find local expertise to maintain the equipment, and travel is sometimes restricted. But the sacrifices have produced great results, and many people have been saved. As a matter of fact, there have been so many witch doctors in Haiti saved that the folks at FBN have lost count.

After the Gulf War in Iraq, FBN had the opportunity to temporarily broadcast over this ancient Biblical land during the transitional government. Once permanent government was reestablished, they had the opportunity to assist in the establishment of another radio ministry which now broadcasts Christian programming in the native language.

Brother Dave Robinson, the radio engineer at FBN, devised suitcase transmitters, and FBN programming was carried into many places. Now with the Internet and phone apps, the signal has been received and acknowledged in nearly every known country and territory. Some of these countries are completely closed to gospel missionaries otherwise

WOTJ had indeed turned into a "mother station" as God answered Clyde Eborn's prayers. The Fundamental Broadcasting Network had been born and was exhibiting healthy growth. However, growing years are also years of overcoming obstacles, and FBN still had a major hurdle to clear in their future.

Chapter Fifteen
1995 - Moving WOTJ/FBN

After all the miracles that God did in saving Clyde Eborn, establishing Grace Baptist Church, WOTJ, and then the Fundamental Broadcasting Network, God showed Himself to be the Almighty once again in 1995 when the station was forced to relocate. The Grace Baptist Church/WOTJ campus sat at the intersection of Country Club Road and Bridges Street in Morehead City. The city is waterlocked with Bogue Sound on one side and a large bay where the Newport River enters the Atlantic Ocean on the other side. Highway 70 (which is called Arendell Street in town) was the only four-lane street running the length of the town. In the summer it was heavily congested as tourists made their way to Atlantic Beach, Emerald Isle, and the small towns "Down East" of Morehead City.

The state's solution was to widen Bridges Street which runs parallel to the congested Arendell Street. Unfortunately, the property where WOTJ's tower was located was required for this expansion project. The state of North Carolina gave the radio station only one year to relocate. Even home owners and business owners would struggle to move that quickly, but moving a radio station involves much more than just a physical relocation. In addition to complying with local regulations, moving a radio tower requires both FAA and FCC approval.

The staff at Grace Baptist and WOTJ scrambled. After a time of prayer one day, Pastor Eborn walked out into the hallway and said, "Fellows, I've got peace from God. I don't know all the answers yet. I don't know how we're going to make this move, but I've got peace. Let's leave it in God's hands." They followed that peace which passes understanding, and God put together the pieces. They located a spacious piece of property with several acres in nearby Newport. It had already been cleared of timber by developers who were planning to build an apartment complex.

They met the developers under a pecan tree on the property, spread the maps on the hood of a pickup truck, and discussed the purchase. The property was in two lots and they needed both. When the developers suggested that they make an offer, they offered all they felt they could afford. The response was a hearty laugh. But, after some haggling, they settled on a price. Knowing the time crunch they were in, God once again moved, and the developers allowed them to begin construction on the radio tower pad and transmitter building even before their loan was approved.

God also gave them favor with the FCC, the FAA, and the planning department of the city of Newport; and the effects of mountain moving faith were seen once again. This time, the mountain of paperwork associated with governmental regulations was moved through in a timely fashion by the mighty hand of God.

In addition to paperwork and approvals, all the equipment had to be physically relocated. They moved everything they could relocate without shutting down while the signal was still being broadcast from Morehead City. Then they went off the air in Morehead City, moved the transmitter and the last of the equipment with an efficiency that would do a military unit proud, and came back on the air in Newport within a day's time.

As they sold off the Morehead City property, God showed His favor upon them one more time by providing them with a fair settlement from the state for the portion of their property that was needed for the road construction. He also helped them with selling the remainder of the Morehead City property to another church at a reasonable price.

The Fundamental Broadcasting Network with its multiple stations, affiliates, translators, internet feed, and phone apps has received responses from over 230 countries and territories. They have numerous testimonies on file from people who have been saved and from saints who have been edified by FBN's broadcasts.

It started with a humble soul winner giving a <u>What Must I Do to Be Saved</u>? tract to a coworker. This led to the salvation of a young production worker who God raised up to be a spiritual leader. Through that soul-minded leader, God raised up the Grace Baptist Church, the WOTJ Christian Radio station, and the Fundamental Broadcasting Network. Clyde Eborn also served as one of the four founding members of World Wide New Testament Baptist Missions. Hundreds of thousands if not millions have heard the gospel.

Pastor Clyde Eborn graduated to heaven May 7, 2022, but he has not yet received his full reward. According to Revelation 22:12 that reward will be given when Jesus returns. It could not be given upon Clyde Eborn's arrival in heaven because "***to some extent, that revival continues until this day...***" No doubt, the work of Grace Baptist Church, WOTJ, World Wide New Testament Baptist Missions, and the Fundamental Broadcasting Network will be causing credits to be added to his account daily until Jesus comes.

Chapter Sixteen
Odds And Ends

A hundred more chapters could be written if there were enough time to investigate all the great things God has done. Many other noteworthy events were mentioned during the dozens of interviews which provided most of the input to this book. This final chapter will highlight a few of them, and also add a few closing thoughts.

1958 - Gene Myatt Saved

A young man named Gene Myatt worked at DuPont with Pollard, Eborn, and others who had gotten saved. Pollard asked him, "Are you a Christian?" Myatt replied that he was a pretty good fellow, listed things that he didn't do, and said that he didn't believe a person could know for sure if he was going to heaven or not. Pollard told him he was either saved or lost and assured him that he could know. Norm Pollard then gave him a tract. Shortly afterwards, Myatt's dad passed away. The Holy Spirit burned into his heart that someday he would pass away also. He prayed and asked God to save him. When he told Norm Pollard about it, Pollard counseled, "You need to get out of that Methodist church." As Myatt recalled of the church that he had been attending: "No one had ever really got right down to it and told me the facts regarding salvation."

He began attending a Baptist church; then about 1960 he went to help with the planting of Liberty Baptist church in Snow Hill, North Carolina. He became a founding member there, and for over six decades Brother Gene Myatt served as a deacon, treasurer, grounds keeper, and soul winner in that church. He served under both Pastor Robert Joyner and Pastor Ken Bartholomew who were each mentioned earlier. Brother Myatt finally surrendered his grounds keeping job to someone younger when he reached 85 years of age.

1959 - Charlie Anderson Saved

Charlie Anderson was one of the engineers at DuPont and was also the chairman of the deacons in a local Presbyterian church. One day he told his coworker Frank Smith that he would like to see his small Presbyterian church grow. Frank Smith was the same man who would later invite Ellen Mills to church, which resulted in Ernie Mills getting saved, and then starting the Durham Rescue Mission.

In response to Charlie's comment, Frank invited Charlie to go on visitation with him. The Presbyterian deacon went out soul winning with the young Independent Baptist preacher. It was the first time Charlie had experienced confrontational personal soul winning. Although he was uncomfortable with it, he persisted in visiting with his coworker friend each week. He witnessed Frank Smith leading some people to the Lord.

After a while, Frank asked Charlie to do the talking and to try to lead someone to the Lord. At that point, Charlie recognized that he'd never been born again himself. He knew he couldn't lead someone else to do what he himself had not done. However, his pride wouldn't let him publicly admit that he'd never been saved.

Charlie wrestled miserably with the Lord and his pride until Saturday morning when he finally "called upon God to be merciful to me a sinner and save my soul for Jesus' sake." God did save Charlie Anderson, and soon he was called to preach. He joined Eborn, Joyner, Smith, and others who resigned from DuPont to go into the ministry full time. Charlie attended BJU, then either pastored or worked on staff at four Independent Baptist churches. His final pastorate before his homegoing was in Greensboro, North Carolina.

The *"revival continues until this day"* in the Anderson family. All three of his sons serve, or have served, in some form of mission work. Two of his daughters spent part of their careers teaching in Christian schools. All seven of his children are saved and serving the Lord in some way. To the best of Mrs. Anderson's knowledge as of the date of our phone conversation, all 21 grandchildren are saved.

Buster's Van Route

Yet, another example of how the *"revival continues until this day"* is that a man they called Buster would bring a boy named J.T. to Lifegate Baptist Church in the tiny community of Chicod, North Carolina. Buster would pick up J.T. and others for all three services each week in his Ford Econoline van. J.T. Edwards went on to pastor Freedom Baptist Church in nearby Simpson, North Carolina, and Buster became a deacon there.

"Framed Up On"

Some of the preachers from around the Greenville and Kinston areas used a phrase I'd never heard before: "*framed up on.*" Pastor Clyde Eborn said it was part of the reason Charlie Anderson got saved: "...we all framed up on him... we boys framed up on him and started praying... and Charlie got saved." Pastor Bobby Thomas remembered being the milkman for the Carolina Dairy shortly after he got out of the military. He said, "They kind of framed up on me; they were going to pray for the milkman when he came." Framing up on him worked, and Bobby did get saved. He then went on to pastor Calvary Baptist Church of Greenville, North Carolina, for 42 years. It is unknown how these country preachers latched on to this particular phrase, but may God help us to unite with Christian brothers and sisters, and "*frame up on*" some more unsaved souls!

1960 - Another Preacher From DuPont

Norm Pollard usually sat with a group of five or six Christians to eat lunch at DuPont. One unsaved man named Alvis Harris often joined them. Pollard and the others witnessed to Harris and gave him tracts. Harris's wife was also saved and was attending a Free Will Baptist church. He visited her church a few times, then on January 24, 1960, he went to a revival and heard Evangelist Bobby Jackson preach. Harris declined to go forward for the invitation, but after the service the pastor and a deacon stopped by. Alvis Harris got saved that night in his own home. In 1964, he joined the host of preachers who resigned from DuPont to go into the ministry. Harris attended the FWB Bible College in Nashville; and then from 1966 to 1998, he pastored three churches: two in Eastern North Carolina, and one near Charleston South Carolina.

1966 - Even the Great Don't Win Every Battle

Although Norm Pollard won scores of people to the Lord, unfortunately his own mother was not one of them. His son remembers the last time he saw his grandmother. He and Norm took her some groceries around Christmas time, as they did every week. As they were leaving, Norman Pollard looked at his mother and said, "Mother, you need to get things right." She replied, "I'm not ready. I've got plenty of time." They left her, and Norm Pollard never spoke a word all the way home. A few days later she had a stroke. Soon afterwards, they buried her. She was only 53; and as far as they knew, she had been in good health up to that point. Norm Pollard Jr. could not recall his father ever speaking of his mother any more after she passed away. Apparently, it was too painful.

Thankfully, the story was different with his mother's brother. Norm Pollard had led his uncle to the Lord about four years earlier, but then his uncle passed away only one week after Norm's mother passed away. After these two events, Norm would often tell people he was witnessing to, "You don't have time because you don't know when you're going to pass away."

2007 - Everlastingly At It

Norm Pollard never stopped winning souls. Shortly after he retired from DuPont, he was cutting a dead branch from a tree. He fell and broke his back in three places. When Norm Jr. went to visit him in the hospital, he couldn't get in the room because there were so many preachers there. One of them was Dr. Lee Roberson. From that time on, Pollard was disabled to some degree although he still managed to get to church. Later cancer also took its toll and by 2007, he was "shut in." Despite these limitations, he won the guy who cut his grass to the Lord. The guy went down the road singing; and Norm Pollard got his grass cut for $25 a week until he graduated to heaven in 2008.

2021 - Small World

My wife and I were walking the streets of Morehead City, looking for a car show that was supposed to be held in connection with Morehead City's annual Seafood Festival. It turns out we'd been misinformed about the hours of the car show, so we never did find it. But what we did find was a table set up where two men were passing out free Gideon New Testaments. As we chatted with them, it came to light that I was an Independent Baptist preacher. The taller of the two men immediately let me know that he had been saved at People's Baptist Church in Greenville, North Carolina. When I asked if he happened to know Norm Pollard, Robert Jolly's face lit up, and he joyfully exclaimed: "Norm Pollard led me to the Lord!"

As a freshman at East Carolina University, Robert had gone out with some friends and gotten drunk. He had been raised to know better, and Holy Ghost conviction dealt with him (his testimony is amazingly similar to my own in this regard). He sought out a high school buddy that he knew was a Christian and who was also enrolled at ECU. The friend invited him to People's Baptist for the Wednesday evening prayer meeting. Pastor Mosher preached on hell; and by the time the sermon was over, Robert Jolly says he would have been willing to crawl to the altar if that's what it took to get saved. He went forward, and Norman Pollard was the counselor who took him aside and led him to the Lord through the scriptures. That was September 13, 1966. Robert stayed at People's for about a year and went on visitation some with Pollard. After a year, another of Robert's friends had been called to pastor a nearby church, so Robert left People's to help his friend in that ministry. Robert had retired from a career in public education and was serving as a Gideon representative in Eastern North Carolina when we met him.

Satanic Opposition

The men of God interviewed consistently downplayed the opposition they faced as they accomplished their ministries. It seemed they were being careful not to glorify the devil in any way, even when God ultimately gave the victory. But they did face satanic and occultic foes. As Grace Baptist church was building the tower for the radio, their facilities were broken into repeatedly. Deputies found evidence of animal sacrifices in the woods near them. In New Bern, the "Church" and School of Wicca set up camp. At one point, Pastor Wingard debated their leader, Gavin Frost, on a locally televised news program. Thankfully, the school moved away from New Bern some time after that. A Charisma magazine article dated September 30, 2000, linked the exodus of the Wiccans to "gold dust miracles" at two charismatic New Bern churches. Be that as it may, the satanic opposition was real; but God gave the victories.

Oliver B. Greene Tent Revivals.

The impact of Oliver B. Greene's preaching in tent revivals and on the radio has likely been grossly understated in this book. It has been mentioned that Norm Pollard got saved at a tent meeting, and that People's Bible Church was started as a direct result of Greene's tent meetings in Greenville, North Carolina. Grace Baptist Church in Kinston where Ernie Robertson pastored was also reportedly started as a result of an Oliver B. Greene tent revival. Many of the senior saints in Eastern North Carolina are quick to attribute the spirit of revival in this area partly to the influence of Greene's preaching. It was somewhat surprising that relatively few of the trails followed in this book led directly to him. Oliver's brother, Jack Greene, was also greatly used of God in preaching revivals in the churches.

Pastor Robert Winstead

Another man of God who has not been given adequate credit in this book is Pastor Robert Winstead, the fourth of the founders of World Wide New Testament Baptist Missions. By no means is this an intentional slight. Brother Winstead was the first of the four to graduate to heaven, passing away in 2014. This was prior to the research for this book beginning. Another factor is that Trinity Baptist Church of Wilson, which he pastored for 39 years, is a couple hours inland. Also, I knew Pastors Wingard, Eborn, and Bell personally, whereas I only met Brother Winstead one time at the annual Camp Meeting which Trinity Baptist Church hosts each August. To be sure, the accounts of what God did through Pastor Winstead are just as thrilling as those which are documented here, but we'll have to wait to hear those stories in heaven unless someone else documents them.

Meeting Bill Wingard

Most of us would struggle to recall exactly when and where we first met the people who are now our friends. However, it was intriguing to note how many people distinctly remembered the first time they met Pastor Bill Wingard. It has already been noted that Russell Bell recalled their first meeting in the parking lot of Grace Baptist Church in Morehead City when Grace was still meeting in a rented building. It has also been noted that Jack Hunt of Mission Aeroservices recalled immediately bonding with Pastor Wingard at a preacher's fellowship. Bobby Thomas, the pastor of Calvary

Baptist Church in Greenville for 42 years, who had preached the message that so greatly encouraged Ernie Mills, recalled the first time he met Bill Wingard: "He crawled up like a mother hen over me and prayed that God would direct. I feel God heard the man's prayer."

Spontaneously praying with people is something Pastor Wingard was noted for, and Brother Bobby's experience closely parallels my own distinct memories of meeting Preacher Bill for the first time. It was at a funeral, and a mutual friend introduced us. We chatted a couple minutes; then the next thing I knew, his long arm was around my shoulders and he was praying for me and the church that I pastored. Later, I was in a doctor's office and overheard the lady in front of me telling the receptionist that Pastor Wingard had just prayed with her in the parking lot.

But Pastor Wingard did not always make the "mother hen" first impression. Jim Schettler, while serving on the staff of West Coast Baptist College in Lancaster, California, also distinctly remembered meeting Pastor Wingard for the first time. As a young man, Schettler was chaperoning a college singing group. They arrived at Calvary Baptist Church in New Bern on a 4th of July weekend and found Preacher Bill tossing horseshoes with some other men. Schettler informed the preacher that they had arrived, and Pastor Wingard responded: "I thought they were going to send a preacher." Red-faced, Schettler replied, "I am the preacher." Wingard said: "Don't be long." Wingard watched the horseshoes flying through the air the entire time, never making eye contact with Schettler. Decades later, Schettler acknowledged that, as a young man, he was totally intimidated by the austere first impression that Pastor Wingard made on him. However, before that patriotic service was over with, their hearts had begun to knit in Christ; and they held each other in high esteem throughout the years that have followed.

Somehow, whether the first impression was of a "mother hen" or of a stern, austere preacher, Pastor Wingard consistently made a first impression on folks that they never forgot.

Education

It was interesting to note the different levels of education that the men which God chose to use attained. Bill Wingard stopped short of his doctorate, but was later awarded honorary doctorates. Robert Joyner earned degrees through correspondence work. Bud Calvert stopped short of beginning graduate work. Russell Bell spent some time at BJU but never earned a degree. Ernie Mills graduated from a certificate program at BJU, and then was later awarded two honorary doctorates. Clyde Eborn had no formal training. Yet God used each of these men in significant ways. God made clear through the Apostle Paul that He *would not have you to be ignorant...* (I Thessalonians 4:13), yet it is obvious that our education does not have to fit into any one mold. God can use the diligent servant who educates himself in God's Word, regardless of the degree to which man recognizes his education.

God's Timing

For seven years, I felt no liberty to begin writing, yet the memory of Pastor Wingard's comment that, "***to some extent, that revival continues until this day...***" never went away. The thought occurred to me that these men of God were humble enough and feared God enough that they would prefer that no book referring to them be published in their lifetime. It seemed as if they feared they would lose God's blessings on their ministries if anything moved them toward even a passing thought of pride.

147

Then suddenly, my thinking changed to: "If you don't do it now, you'll never be able to do it." It felt like God was giving me liberty to move ahead. The first person I scheduled an interview with was Pastor Bill Wingard. We met on Nov. 19, 2020, and had a blessed time of fellowship as he told the stories of how God had worked in his life. He appeared to be in good health and certainly had a clear mind, but shortly after Thanksgiving it was revealed that he had cancer. He went to heaven on March 12, 2021, just six days short of his 87th birthday, and only four months after we had met.

Then the Covid pandemic hit and for about a year, no interviews were conducted for fear of being a carrier to the senior saints I would need to interview. By December, 2021, I again felt liberty to conduct interviews; and Pastor Clyde Eborn was among the first. We met on December 8, 2021, and again on February 2, 2022. Although he was 92 years old by the time of our second interview, he was vibrant, energetic, and clear minded. It was a shock when he went to heaven after a stroke only three months later on May 7, 2022.

Frank Smith was yet a third example of God's timing. We met on July 29, 2022. His promotion to heaven on October 5, 2022, also occurred less than three months after our meeting. I will be eternally grateful that I had the opportunity to spend some time with these men of God before they departed to their eternal homes! *He that walketh with wise men shall be wise...* (Proverbs 13:20). Don't take lightly the opportunities God provides to learn from seasoned saints!

The Greatest Thing You've Seen God Do

As I interviewed the men and women of God who are spoken of in this book, I developed the habit of asking as the final question:

"What is the one greatest thing you've seen God do?" These folks had just told all these wonderful stories about how God had provided everything from free shipping, to a free airport, to millions of dollars worth of buildings and facilities. Yet, when asked, "What is the one greatest thing you've seen God do?" they inevitably began to talk about souls being saved. Possibly, the conclusion that God would have us to draw from this observation is that He provides best for those who are most focused on eternal souls.

A Final Thought

As I began this book, my primary prayer request was simply that God would forward that vision that evangelist Mike Pelletier had to get God's people praying for revival. As I learned more about how revival actually occurred in Eastern North Carolina, I added a second request to my prayers. I prayed that God would use this book to help more of us to be persistent soul winners like Norm Pollard and to simply *sow beside all waters* (Isaiah 32:20). Thirdly, as I learned the fates of the great ministries God raised up through the men and women whose stories are told here, I became burdened with the fact that each generation has a responsibility to maintain and expand what God started in the previous generations. My final, and overarching, prayer request regarding this book is simply that it will bring glory to God through His answering of the first three prayers.

If this book has helped stir your heart to pray for revival, win souls, and to support and encourage existing ministries, then God has answered my prayers. To God be the glory.

Printed in the USA
CPSIA information can be obtained
at www.ICGtesting.com
CBHW060705100624
9690CB00008B/8

9 781630 734930